I0568802

Journaling

Journal Prompts to Inspire Creativity and Passion

(How to Write a Journal in a Way That Improves Every Aspect of Your Life)

Christy Rondon

Published By **Phil Dawson**

Christy Rondon

All Rights Reserved

Journaling: Journal Prompts to Inspire Creativity and Passion (How to Write a Journal in a Way That Improves Every Aspect of Your Life)

ISBN 978-1-998769-36-0

No part of this guidebook shall be reproduced in any form without permission in writing from the publisher except in the case of brief quotations embodied in critical articles or reviews.

Legal & Disclaimer

Table Of Contents

Chapter 1: Explains Why You Should Do

You Journal? The 7 Benefits Of Journaling

People usually think that journaling is for kids who want to gain a clear view of themselves and how to deal with the stress that middle school brings. Journal writing isn't restricted to teens It has a larger range of applications. It's a method to express yourself and be empowered to understand yourself better. Journaling is a great way to enhance the quality of your life drastically.

Journaling can help people gain insight into their own feelings by expressing their thoughts and thoughts. It's a powerful method of solving problems as it is much easier to come up with solutions when you write things on paper. It's an ideal tool to explore and getting rid of negative emotions. It's beneficial for the overall health of a person. In addition, it's the method of paying attention to specific areas and achieving objectives.

There are numerous proven advantages of journaling. The main benefits are listed below:

Health Benefits

Journaling can help you clear your mind of confusion, and create a link between your emotions, thoughts, and actions, and positively impact your mental health.

It has been established that keeping journals can reduce anxiety and stress, boosts the immune system and memory and improves one's mood. This is especially beneficial for people who have been through the trauma of a lifetime.

How to deal with depression

Journaling aids people in managing their depression because it helps them release the negative emotions. It is a way to heal by writing down your thoughts on paper. The reason behind an unhappiness or negative emotion can be identified clearer when it's not lingering in your mind.

Journaling can aid students in college who are prone to depression to reduce their anxiety and rumination. These are two of the contributing elements of depression symptoms." (Gortner, Rude, & Pennebacker, 2006).

Reduce Anxiety

Barbara Markway, a psychologist She has stated "There's nothing better to understand your thinking process than to record your thoughts on paper." (Ackerman 2019). In her opinion, to tackle your problematic thoughts, you need first recognize the patterns. Journaling is a way to acknowledge the negative internal dialogue going on in you and to discover the root of your anxiety.

Writing can reduce anxiety because it:

* Relaxes and clears your mind.

* Releases buried emotions and tension.

* Helps release negative thoughts.

Allows you to discover your anxiety-ridden moments.

* Provides you with the opportunity to write down your accomplishments as well as your struggles.

* Enhances self-awareness, enables you recognize your triggers.

It makes it easier to monitor your progress as you go through treatments. (Ackerman, 2019)

Stress Management

Stress is a problem that all of us will have to face at some moment in our lives. It's hard to stay away from stress in our modern society, however there are ways to lessen the effect that it has on your daily life. Journaling is one such method. Writing down your thoughts helps to understand your particular stress triggers, so that you can work to reduce them.

An investigation has revealed that writing expressively like journaling can improve liver function and reduce the blood pressure of a person.

Journaling can be helpful in managing stress due to the fact that it:

* Helps reduce the symptoms of certain illnesses.

* Improves cognitive functioning.

* Strengthens the immune system.

It allows you to look at your thinking and change your viewpoint.

* Decreases rumination and enccurages actions.

* Provides you with the opportunity to plan your move and take into consideration the potential possibilities. (Ackerman, 2019)

Healing Impact

Journaling is a crucial element in the process of recovery. Writing can help you recover from the negative effects of a disorder, habit or even an incident. "If you're struggling in following a traumatizing incident Journaling can help to see the positive side of things. It may even aid in seeing the positives of the trauma, which can help to reduce the severity of effects that may accompany trauma." (Ullrich and Lutgendorf 2002) (Ackerman 2019)

Journaling helps you face your challenges instead of avoiding them. It allows you reflect on the experiences you have had and strengthens your identity. Additionally, it can have an emotional impact. A gratitude journal is especially beneficial to help recover.

Better Productivity

Journaling is a great instrument for setting goals and time management, organizing and tracking progress. In essence, it is about reflecting on, planning, and planning. You can try bullet journaling as an innovative and customizable method of planning goals and projects. We'll talk further about bullet journaling in the future.

Goal Setting

Setting goals might seem like something that is easy but it requires a certain amount of expertise to set the proper objectives and a lot of discipline to stick to achieve these goals.

You can write the goals you have set within your diary. It could serve as your central point of reference for your long-term and short-term goals. A study carried out at the Dominican University showed that those who record their goals stand a better chance of reaching them than those who don't record them down. (Hicks, 2016)

The act of writing down your goals gives you with the chance to make informed decisions about what they should look like. By writing your goals down on paper, you prove that they're what you truly desire. When they're written down, they are something like a personal agreement that you've signed with yourself. You have a clear idea of what you'd like to accomplish and the steps you must follow to achieve it. Every time you open your journal you're constantly reminded of your goals. You are able to constantly review your progress to ensure that your goals are in line with your goals of your life.

Organization

Journals can be used to organize your work in a systematic way. Note down things that require immediate attention and need to be completed. For instance, if you are applying to an institution, you could take note of the essays you need to write. If you plan to launch an enterprise, you're capable of arranging your priorities and can help you save time and cash.

Monitoring Progress

You can assess your productivity and progress by analyzing:

What are the tasks that were completed?

* How long did you spend on these tasks?

What tasks remain on the list?

What factors increase or decrease your efficiency?

* When are you the most or least productive throughout the day?

Express Yourself

Everybody can have bad days. It's normal to be distracted and less productive during the day. The situation could get worse when you must finish a certain project that day.

A journal can be very helpful to help you deal with these occasions. It is a great way to write about negative emotions you are experiencing. If you are able to express yourself in a way that makes you feel sad or frustrated that can have a therapeutic effect.

The act of writing down your feelings in a journal can save you from accidentally unleashing your anger to your spouse, family members or any other innocent person. In addition, once you've written and removing your emotional burden , you'll be able to perform your everyday activities with ease.

Motivator's Source

It is possible to save a few pages to write inspiring words or quotes. Some prefer writing affirmations such as:

* I am smart and able.

* I lead a tranquil and harmonious lifestyle.

It is useful for reference

When you have a time frame, when you revisit and look through your journal, you can observe how you've grown as well as the challenges you've conquered, and which remain. You might be pleased to see that your goals have been achieved. If you have some goals that haven't been met, you can look into the causes to the reason. For example, was the goal too lofty? Did you choose the wrong strategy? Was there something you could have different done?

Creativity is Increasing

Journals are a great way to write down your own ideas of creativity as well as ideas you encounter when you meet people or go to a new location. This way your thoughts are in one place and you can apply them when you have to think creatively. It is also possible to find links between the notes, and mix two seemingly different ideas together. This method has the potential to improve your ability to generate innovative ideas.

Journaling can also give you the opportunity to gain insight into you subconscious. When you are in the state of meditation you'll be able to dig deeper into your mind and uncover aspects of your unconscious which aren't normally easily accessible to you. These new insights can be further explored with your journal, and then used to create creativity.

In addition, you can employ your imagination to make your journal distinctive. For instance, you could utilize highlighters, stickers or calligraphy. You can use your creative talents and add your preferred accessories. Coloring the sections or drawing are other options that can be interesting.

Better Understanding of Yourself

Journaling gives you the time and space to think about yourself. It helps you understand your strengths and weaknesses. It will help you discern certain aspects, such as your thinking patterns and the root causes of your actions and emotions as well as some contradictions that you may have in your life.

A Better Understanding of Your Exper ences

The truth is that the experiences we have define us as individuals. Journaling gives us the chance to think about our own experiences. We all have the experience of being in a way that was not our style or making a choice that we regret. These kinds of situations are best explored in journals.

They can help us gain an understanding of the reasons we react to certain circumstances either in a positive or negative way.

As you begin to document your experiences, you could begin to recognize common themes among them, which can lead to the realization of life lessons that could not otherwise be found. The lessons learned can then be relied upon if you ever find yourself experiencing similar scenarios in the near future.

Writing down your experience by keeping a journal allows you to focus more to your relationships with people you interact with. Arguments with your spouse could be solved much more quickly if you make the effort to write about it and discover the root of the reason you believe you were wronged.

Make Your Senses Sharper

Journaling can improve your the capacity to think critically and observe. It helps you see things in a completely different perspective. It allows you to find your individuality and build self-awareness. If you keep a journal keeping a journal You begin to observe things with greater attention, something you may not otherwise have. You are more likely to look at positive and negative aspects of every situation. You find beauty everywhere, which you might not have before. Your emotional intelligence grows when you become more aware with your own motives and the motives of the people around you.

Journaling, in other words, can help you gain better understanding of life.

Record Your Memories

People are prone to forgetting things fast. If, for instance, you ask someone about what you did specific day in the month of March you might have a hard time being able provide many details. However, if you ask them about what they did today and they might have plenty to share with you.

It's tragic how we often lose track of our past experiences. The pace of life is swift and before we know it, memories are all we have left. Journaling can come as a way to capture memories that might otherwise have be lost in the ages.

We are living in the age of social media, and memories can be easily captured as photographs. But the benefit of keeping a journal is that memories can be documented by you own viewpoint. Journals allow you to also provide more depth when you are examining your feelings, thoughts, and thoughts, something that's not present on your standard Facebook profile.

Similar to that, you might go to a variety of stunning locations in your life, however, you may forget about them when the vacation is done. If you keep an account of your travels, you'll be able to remember these experiences throughout your life. Journals are a way to keep track about your experiences. It helps you keep your experiences. While it's beneficial in the moment however, it is worthless in the near future.

Each of the advantages mentioned in this chapter could be effective on its individual merits, but when they are combined they can help you build the foundation for an incredible life. They help you break free and take charge of your life. This is the reason why journaling is an effective tool.

It's important to remember that what benefits you reap from journaling are contingent on your personality, the kind of journaling you decide to perform, and what you hope to gain from this method. In Chapter 3, we'll look at the different ways of journaling as well as the distinct benefits they each bring.

Getting Started

Journaling is a wonderful activity in that it's extremely accessible. It doesn't require fancy equipment or expensive purchase. All you require is a surface to write on and a pen.

Keep things as easy as you can. The more complicated the procedure the less likely you'll ever be able to start. That being said don't be cheap or lazy. Purchase a notebook and stationery that you appreciate and which meets your requirements. Make sure you are proud of your notebooking system.

In addition, journaling doesn't require lengthy writing just. Visual thinkers can sketch out diagrams, sketches charts, mind maps and charts. It is also possible to include snippets from different sources, photos or magazine cut-outs within your journal. This is particularly true in the event that you choose to create your journal online, where you can access every resource available online. In this case you could also include audio and video filesas well.

Let's review some of the tools you could need to consider using to start.

Different types of notebooks or journals

Your personal preferences will be the deciding factor when it comes to deciding which journals or notebooks you would like to use. Many people like journals that are attractive, and some prefer functional. You might, for instance, like writing in a notebook bound that is able to be used for years and the cover is beautiful or even a loose notebook that allows you to exercise more freedom. You might prefer writing on a huge sketch pador discover that a small pocket notebook is better for you because it is able to go with you wherever you travel.

Different Features

Here are some of the things be aware of when buying journals.

Note: Notebooks are offered in a variety of sizes. The most frequently used sizes are B6 and A4. Certain brands, like Moleskine, offer unique, custom-designed sizing. Milligram is the name used to describe the sizes of notebooks in centimeters on the notebook's listing. This means that you can view the measurements and purchase the one that is most appropriate to meet your requirements.

Sheets and pages Notebooks are created using sheets of paper. One sheet makes two pages. If a book is larger in pages, it is likely to be heavier and thicker. Therefore, if you wish to carry it around with you it is possible to choose an easier version with smaller pages. But, the majority of people prefer a more substantial notebook, which is more mobile, but that lasts longer. A heavy and thick notebook comes with the physical benefit of appearing more significant. This increases the likelihood to be taking the process of journaling seriously.

* The weight on the surface: You will determine the weight of the paper by it's GSM which is grams for each square meter. Paper that is heavier or thicker is thought to be more durable due to the fact that when you use pen, your writing doesn't bleed through the paper on opposite side. It's worth considering slightly thicker papers if you like the design the journal.

* Page layout and rules Notebooks are equipped with the standard rules of 7 mm. They also come with different measurements for rulings, like 6mm or 8mm. You could also utilize a notebook with dot grid or grid or a special French rulings, or even simply a notebook.

Covers: Typically notebooks come with covers that are a little heavier that the paper. They could be printed, textured, or plain. Certain books come with heavier covers constructed of leather, for instance,

Classic Moleskine and Midori Travelers Notebooks.

* Ideal for fountain pens The release of more ink by fountain pen. This could cause some types of paper. Therefore, it is recommended to take a look at the listing of products and make sure the paper you purchase is suitable. Rhodia and Clairefontaine brands make fountain pen-friendly notebooks, and Moleskine has this type of paper in their sketchbook range or the art range.

* Recycled and acid-free paper It is recommended to make use of white paper bleached, and has been treated with acid. What is drawn or written on such paper can last for a lengthy period of time. This makes it appropriate for journals and diaries that have to endure the test of time.

The majority of recycled paper is not coated. It is eco-friendly and has a classic style that appeals to some, however it might not be suitable for people who write using fountain pen.

Closers: Certain notebooks which are contained in a compendium or an outer cover have closures with elastics that aid in keeping their condition in top shape. Delfonics, Rhodia, and Moleskine are among the brands that sell notebooks that have closures with elastic.

"Bindings". The process of binding determines how durable the book is as well as how flat it lies and how sturdy the pages are, as well as whether they can be removed easily. You can select the type of binding that best suits the manner you intend to utilize your notebook.

Binding with glue is not particularly safe. However, some books, like sketchbooks are bound with glue to ensure you can easily remove the pages with ease.

Thin notebooks that can hold at least 64 pages can be bound using staples. A larger number of pages may be stitched by stitched binding. This kind of binding is stronger.

Notebooks are tightly bound with thread and glue. The notebooks can also be laid on the floor. They're a great option for those who prefer to use a notebook that is stylish and also has strong binding.

Certain books are bound with spiral wires. These are also known for their spiral notebooks. They might be easier for you if you wish to eliminate pages. For the majority of people who write, taking out pages is considered to be counterproductive however, this is a matter that you can decide.

* Handmade or mass-produced Notebooks are produced in mass quantities by large companies, but also made by people who love creating books. Hand-made books are generally constructed of high-quality paper. They might have unique features , such as hand printing and letterpress. But, they could cost more. They can also be of high-quality such as those published under Rhodia and the Clairefontaine or Rhodia brands.

The benefit of using notebooks that are physical is that you must slow down when writing, which allows you more time to think. Your writing style expresses your mood and your emotions in a way. Many people believe that it is more personal feel when you write your thoughts down on paper.

The downside of using notebooks that are physical is that you will need to protect them from the eyes of others, making it harder to safeguard your privacy. Another issue is that they are more likely to be damaged or stolen. This is especially the case in cases where your lifestyle is less steady, as for instance, when you travel frequently or don't have a stable base of operations.

Different types of writing equipment

There are plenty of alternatives when it comes down to writing tools. You can choose to use any of your favourite highlighters, fine-tip pens or markers from brands such as Pilot, Faber Castell, Sakura, Crayola, Steadtler and Tombow. If you're interested, you could add other accessories, like a ruler and bullet journal stencils stamps, stickers as well as correction tape whiteout tape, washi tape as well as binder clip.

Pen vs. Pencil

Pens are better than using a pencil since it is clearer, more legible and lasts for longer. However, if the pen isn't high-quality it could leave streaks of ink, and the writing might become stained. If you're unable to remember and have to erase words, your work may look messy.

The benefits of pencils is that it can bring back the pleasure of the early school when you were able to write using it. Furthermore you can erase and correct mistakes quickly. It is not necessary to remove words in order that it's more neat. However the writing could appear to be dull, and disappear after a while. If you draw with a pencil, make sure you sharpen it regularly. A sharp pencil can ruin the uniform look in your notebook.

Colored Gel Pens

It's a great option to utilize colored gel pen. They can help make your journal look more appealing, and can also provide a unique expression when you use a variety of shades. The use of different colors is beneficial for highlighting specific sections of your journal that you consider to be essential or for organizing parts of your journal on the color coded system. Be cautious when choosing the right pens to the kind of paper you're using.

Digital Journals

There are numerous journaling software. Microsoft OneNote for devices with digital capabilities is an excellent choice. It's a note-taking application that lets you take any information you want to on a digital canvas and place it in any location. It allows you to write using stylus or type handwritten pages, scan handwritten notes, or even clip an online page. It arranges your content with virtual notebooks, which provide more versatility than a traditional paper notebook.

There are a lot of journaling apps , such as:

"Day One" features an intuitive interface , and is accessible for Android, iOS, and Mac.

Diarium: You could make use of it to dictate the journal entry either Windows as well as Android.

*Glimpses You have Windows and you want to use free journaling, you can download this application.

* Journey: It can access Journey for journaling on Windows, Mac, Android, Web, iOS, and Chrome OS to journal.

* Penzu, Momento, and Grid Diary are some other useful applications.

The benefit of keeping journals in digital format is that it's more secure. It is able to be kept for longer. It's versatile. It is easy to arrange and organize what you've written. It's also neater looking.

It is simple to create entries using journaling software. There are a variety of applications that provide a pleasing interface that makes journaling fun. You can set reminders that are automatic and also export your journal entries to be accessed by other applications.

You can sync your journal to ensure it's constantly updated on different devices. Journaling prompts can be added photographs, photos, weather, and even locations.

However, the spontaneity and spontaneity that comes with journaling could be lost in the event that you are caught in the trap of over editing it is a simple task to perform when using a journal that is digital. Additionally, the whole process can become more mechanical or boring. A sufficient amount of time is not focused on reflection and thinking in the same way as when using the traditional journal.

Voice Recorder

If you find it's more enjoyable to speak rather than write, take notes in audio format and then transcribing later. To do this, you could make use of a voice recorder or a mobile phone that can do this.

Chapter 2: Methods For Journaling

Journaling is a method that assists you comprehend and manage aspects of your own life and all the things around you. It is also a general concept and can have different aspects based on the specific method or techniques you decide to use.

But, what must be understood and organized can differ from one person to the next. A CEO of the Fortune 500 company will have different requirements from an artist struggling to make ends meet. need different requirements than an at-home mom. This is where the choice of your journaling technique or method can be a challenge.

Types of Journaling

Reflective Journaling

Journaling for reflection is mostly used to analyze past events and actions. You can record every good or bad thing that you have experienced in your life and the implications it has for you. It is also possible to write down what you took away from it.

The benefits of this form of journaling include:

It offers an overview of the situation. It provides a thorough explanation of all the details of what happened that occurred, such as what the event's goal was as well as the people in attendance, and the way you were feeling about the event.

* It helps you consider the reason for how they are. This improves your thinking abilities.

Reflection assists you to understand things and to decide if you want to keep the same values and plan of action in the future or take a decision differently.

* It assists you to take a break from the stress of your thoughts that are numb and help you resolve issues from the past.

* You could even write about what you wrote and ask for the opinion of other people. This will allow you to gain a better

understanding of the issues and make sense of you more clearly.

Mindfulness Journaling

The primary purpose of this journal is to reconnect to your current self. However, you can also use an mindfulness journal to reflect about the past and future. This kind of journaling can allow you to be honest in your inner dialog. It assists you in getting acquainted with your thinking patterns and triggers for emotion. It is a great tool to help you meditate.

You are more aware of the events happening in the world around you. You can write down the events or thoughts, and take on the challenges of life and gain insight from your experiences, and share your gratitude.

It allows you to express your feelings without fearof judgement or expectations. It helps you develop self-compassion, and to concentrate on your personal life. Additionally, it offers positive therapeutic effects. It can lead to improvements in health and recovery.

Bullet Journaling

Bullet journals can help you to increase your productivity , and help you achieve your personal and professional goals. It is a great method of journaling to plan the future, make lists, identify your goals, arrange your daily life and keep track of your progress.

It is distinct from conventional planners in that it prompts the author to think about the way they perceive their responsibilities, tasks, and objectives. It is a process of reflection on a daily as well as a monthly and annual basis rather than making a checklist that is standard.

Before you begin this form of journaling, identify the obstacles you're facing and why you'd like to keep your bullet journal.

The journal also contains:

* Index: It is located at the start of the book. It has pages numbers.

• Future journal: It's a year-long calendar which includes goals for the future activities, tasks, and dates.

A monthly journal: This contains a month-long calendar.

• Daily journal: This lists the tasks to be completed each day.

You can use the speedy recording feature to make use of keywords and phrases that are short instead of complete sentences. This will help make it easier to save time and improve effectiveness. It is also possible to use symbols to create sections that can be known as collections that are in alignment with your long- and short-term objectives.

Journaling Methods

Gratitude Journal

The research in neuroscience has shown that when someone is happy, dopamine and serotonin are released by the brain. The former triggers the brain's pleasure center, and the latter causes the person to feel great. Thus, gratitude is an antidepressant.

The brain is unable to focus on both positive and negative things at the same time. If you're grateful it helps you to stop being unhappy over what you don't have and begin to feel grateful with what you have. Thus, when you keep the gratitude journal and write in your journal all the things you are thankful for, you will become happier.

Creative Journal

Creative journaling is a great option for creative individuals such as writers or artists, as well as graphic designers. It is designed to help individuals to think of ideas, develop creativity, and resolve issues.

The advantages of this journal include:

* It can be used to serve various uses. It can be used as a daily planner notebook, scrapbook, notebook or sketchbook.

* It is possible to use it to develop and improve your abilities. In general, creativity doesn't happen naturally, therefore you require some time to practice.

If you're finding that it hard to think of innovative ideas, make use of this journal to think about ideas.

* It prevents your inner critic from becoming an obstacle to stop your creativity from flourishing since it gives you a place

where you can express your thoughts without fear of being judged or evaluated.

Fitness Journal

A fitness journal will help you set and achieve your fitness and health goals. It is possible to use this kind of journal to see what's working and not working for you and also to determine the activities you'll be taking when you go to the fitness center. It helps eliminate any guesswork. It is possible to get the most outcomes from your exercise routines because you are working to the proper direction. It is also possible to use a type journal to organize your schedule and track your food habits.

Dream Journal

Dream journals help you recall your dreams and to work with the dreams you have. The process of writing down your dreams might require some time since there may be times that you wake up and you are unable to recall the dream. It's best to keep the journal along with the pen near your bed to ensure you can write down the entire details of the dream prior to when you forget the details. If you are on a hectic schedule in the morning and can't write an extensive report, write down the key pictures and the emotions described in your dream. You can further flesh in the specifics later, using the prompts provided to assist you.

Noting down your dreams helps you discover patterns and use them to examine the subconscious thoughts of your mind. A lot of people use dream journaling as a method to attain lucid dreams, an experience where you become aware that you're it is an actual dream.

Reading Journal

The journal can be used to record more than just reading books. You can document your learning experiences using videos and other sources online, too. There are numerous benefits to keeping a journal of reading for example:

* It can help increase retention.

It also allows students to go back and review notes about what they've learned at any point in time.

* It forces an individual to consider and formulate their ideas on what they've read.

* It provides the reader with an opportunity to examine the material they are reading from the perspective of the writer.

* It is a method to practice writing.

After reading, notate the title as well as the names of the author and the publisher. This can be useful to you should you want to be an author. Note the dates when you began and ended your reading. Keep track of the pages. This will allow you to determine the speed of the book. Write a short review or description so you will be able to recall the primary content of the text when you revisit the journal in the future. If you're reading a novel, you may write a few sentences on the plot themes, setting, and the characters. After you've read poetry, you'll be able to write about the structure, imagery as well as the language and flow.

Project Journal

The keeping of a journal to aid in managing projects comes with numerous advantages. These include:

* You get a more complete view; it allows individuals to consider their work from different angles. You can look at things from the stakeholder's perspectives.

* You can make a plan for your next steps. You can look over your journal to gain a better understanding of the progress made on the project. On this basis, you can outline and record the next steps to be done.

* You can organise your thoughts. When your thoughts on a particular project are documented, connections between them start to appear and things become easier to see. Writing can help organize thoughts.

* You are able to deal with issues more efficiently. In order to resolve any issue, you need to first identify it. You must reflect on and refining your issue in phrases before making any attempts to solve the issue.

* You can learn from your mistakes for your future projects. It is possible to note the things that worked and the ones that didn't perform. Which are things you might have changed?

One Sentence Journal

This technique is ideal for those who don't have time for themselves. There are many who are unable to incorporate journaling into their hectic schedules, but they shouldn't be left out of the advantages of journaling. Journalists can write one line about what they have experienced during the past 24 hours and keep it in this journal.

The advantage of an all-in-one diary is the fact that it takes virtually no effort or time since you only write one sentence per day. It also means that it's easy to go at the previous entries to have a complete view of the way your life is developing.

Morning Pages

The morning pages involve writing three stream of consciousness pages each day. The goal of the early morning pages is put the thoughts of your mind down quickly and without filtering your thoughts. It's crucial not to get caught up in it, simply take notes of whatever thoughts come to your mind.

This technique was created to help artists overcome blocks to creativity. However, the impact and power of the morning pages are not just limited to artistic activities. It's effective in all aspects of life, such as the marriage or parenting. It is ideal for anyone who seeks clarity, focus and direction in their lives.

This technique can have the effect of clearing space in your head for the most essential things, which helps reduce anxiety and feelings of feeling overwhelmed. New ideas and innovative ways of seeing the world may also come to light through this journaling technique.

The methods listed above are all you have to know about getting started. Select one that is appealing to you and begin writing. As you get more comfortable in journaling, you might consider making your own personal journaling method by combining a few of the methods for journaling found in this guide.

Some examples include:

An appreciation journal can be part of the mindful journaling.

* Project and fitness journaling are both great with the standard bullet journal.

Then, at the end of the day this journal is yours only, so make sure you make sure you write it in a manner you believe will be able bring you the most value.

Chapter 3: Eight Tips For Effective

Journaling

Take a moment to meditate before beginning

No matter what method of journaling you employ, it's important to be relaxed and calm prior to beginning. You can accomplish this by doing some breathing exercises , or simply take a few moments to relax your eyes and connect with your inner self. You can do this using visualization or meditate while listening to some soothing music that plays as background.

Furthermore, it is recommended to pick a place that is quiet, that is free of distractions, and less likelihood of interruptions. It is a place where you can relax and be upright.

If you can close the eyes for couple of minutes and connect with yourself, you'll be in a good position to write effectively. You can think about the things you want to write about. After this, you'll be able to be honest in your writing.

Map Out Ideas

After your meditation , you might decide to sketch out the ideas that came to mind. Do this prior to writing your journal. This is useful when you are planning to write on a particular topic. You can, for instance, write about any subject you find interesting , like the future or work, school, or even cooking. Also, limit yourself to only a few minutes writing about this, but don't let yourself become overwhelmed.

Write as Fast as you can

After a short reflection and brainstorming session, you'll need to begin writing as soon as you can. The most important thing is to write some words written down. Keep moving your pen, and let you thoughts flow freely without allowing your inner critic or censor to stifle your progress.

It is possible to begin by writing about what's taking place in the present or a sensation you're experiencing, such as "I'm so happy about." ...'. Or, you can start with a narrative such as "Astonishing things happened today." ...'.

This can help overcome the initially a writer's block. Once you have your words down, it is more easy to write. When you begin writing, do not return to modify anything. Don't get caught up in over thinking. Let the words flow freely.

However, this recommendation is largely contingent on the kind of journaling you're using. For a bullet journal, for instance, requires you to think carefully about what you will put down on paper , and could require editing as well.

Write Clearly and Clearly

One of the most common mistakes you make when journaling is to try to be perfect in your writing. There isn't a specific format or format of writing that needs to be adhered to. Remember this journal will be only for only you and only you. Therefore, feel at ease writing according to the style it comes to you naturally. Be sure to not appeal to a readership that won't ever read your journal.

Try to be as authentic as you can. The more sincere yourself, the more influential your journal will become. Do not view your personal honesty as a opponent, or something to be embarrassed about. You are free to share your real feelings.

Always mark your entry with a date.

It is a good habit to write down the date each time you make a note in your journal. This will allow you keep an eye on your progress and will make it easier to locate old entries. It will help you recreate the journal chronologically based on the dates. It will also reveal the times you didn't enter a note. Additionally, you'll be aware of what you felt like at various occasions throughout your lifetime.

Title Your Entry

This gives the writing a distinct topic and makes it easier to be referenced later on. The addition of a title to entries can help keep the writing in focus. It is not necessary to come up with the title in advance. You can choose an appropriate title once you have finished your entry. A catchy title can make journals more attractive and interesting.

Re-read and review

After you have finished your journaling After you've finished your journaling session, spend a few minutes to read your journal entries. After that, you should write some sentences to summarize your journal for the day to help you organize it in your head. This helps you recall and then act on the information you've recorded. This is where the real changes take place.

It is possible to keep it and revisit it later. It could provide valuable knowledge.

Enjoy It

Remember to view your journaling as something you wish to do and not something you need to complete. That is take the time to approach it with a positive mindset. Doing this on its own will greatly improve how your journals are written, and will make writing much simpler.

Additionally, there aren't specific rules to journaling. It is possible to write however you find the most satisfying for you. Allow yourself to be free of stress and create a fulfilling and therapeutic experience. Make journaling enjoyable and something enjoyable instead of being a chore.

Chapter 4: Eleven Journal Writing

Strategies

Journals can be used to serve a variety of purposes. It could be a diary of your day-to-day activities in life, your experiences and even your personal memories. It could also be centered around a specific issue, such as current events and your backyard. It could also be used to record your dreams, or for collecting ideas for fiction and poetry.

For ideas and inspiration for your write, you can employ the strategies below.

Take a walk

You can take an outing to draw inspiration from the surroundings. You can write about the concrete objects you observe. You could write about the neighborhood, buildings, the pavement and nature of the area that you are walking in, flowers, birds, plants or even the weather. It is possible to be motivated to write about intangibles like scents, sounds or how you feel.

Sit in a public place and watch the world around you. It's incredible how you can get valuable insight into people and the world around you by taking the opportunity to watch. These insights can later be documented in your journal to gain a better understanding of your personal life.

Explore themes

Choose a general theme and investigate it. For example, you can choose the theme of fear and break it down into subcategories, such as:

* Things that you are afraid of

Things to do when you're afraid

* Strategies to overcome fears

This can be further divided into more specific categories.

"Things that you're scared of' could be subdivided into:

* Be afraid of specific types of people

* Fearful of failure

* Nightmares

* Fears that are not rational

* Horror films

You can make use of all the items mentioned above as topics for journal writing. This way you will be able to get ideas employing this method.

Concentrate on the Senses

One of the best ways to develop the depth of the journal is paying attention to your senses. It is important to pay all your attention to only one sense faculty at one time.

You could, for instance, decide to write about anything that you notice in the surrounding area. It is possible to begin by noticing things in general and then shift your focus on the particular details of these objects, such as the form and material, colours, and so on.

You can also opt to pay attention to the sounds that you hear. Take a moment to close your eyes, and start to listen for the sounds taking all around you. These are typically sounds that are normally overlooked. Pay attention to the sounds of the cars passing from your window, or the tinny sound of your refrigerator.

The goal of this exercise isn't solely to document your experience in a direct way but rather to enhance the ability of you to go beyond the surface of your experience to go further. After a few weeks of practice, you'll find that you can write in greater detail when you write in your journal, as you observe and appreciate the greater degree of subtlety that you experience in your daily experiences.

Past EVENTS

Sit in a quiet place and close your eyes. imagine an event that occurred in the past. It may be a small event or a life-changing event. Make sure to imagine the situation or event in the most detail feasible. Relive the event like you were there. Take note of the things you did as well as how you felt through this moment.

Once you've thought about the event in detail you can now open your eyes to begin writing. Record your impressions of the event, based on the image you created and then take an hour analyzing the events. A few questions you could ask yourself include:

What made you do the way you did?

What made you feel the same way?

What else did people do and what was their motivation?

What are the lessons you can take from this experience? These will help you become a more adept in your future?

Perhaps you can recall your first experience when you gave presentations in school. You can examine the causes of the success or failing. It could be a time that the job you were working on was terminated, something important happened or you might have experienced certain changes in your personal life. These are only a few examples of the kind of things that you could write about.

Be aware that often the most beneficial instances to study are those that you experience the greatest resistance to confronting. The negative experiences you have had could hold the key to changing your life today.

Goals

Think about your dreams, goals and strategies for the future. what are you truly hoping for?

It can be beneficial to imagine your ideal life and keep a journal of what comes to mind. Imagine your goals for your career and the ideal lifestyle you would like to live. You can draw inspiration from each of these topics as journaling for inspiration.

Free Write

This method is extremely useful to overcome writer's block. Set an alarm and then keep the pen moving until the timer stops. Write down the first thought that pops into your mind without limit. If you are unable to think of something to write about You can write "I don't have anything to write," again and again until you have some ideas.

When you begin writing, Do not analyze or judge your work. Your thoughts and writing flow naturally. It's not important to think about whether the thought makes sense or not.

This will allow your mind relax, and fresh ideas will begin to come out of your subconscious mind.

Music

There are many ways to utilize music to aid in the writing process. A simple playlist of music as you write will help you to be inspired. Consider music and see whether it triggers any emotions, thoughts of the past or dreams for the near future.

You can also perform some instrumental music and then write down the lyrics you think fit to the musical mood. Music is an instrument that is well-known to stimulate creativity.

Visual Aids

Make use of visual aids such as videos or images to help you come up with thoughts for journal writing.

For example, you could examine a picture from your childhood and then write about the memories related to the photo. It is also possible to look through Google images to see if something pops out and then utilize this image to inspire new ideas.

Video can also be a fantastic visual aid to journal. Take a look at a video and write down what you've observed. Think about what lessons or ideas can you learn out of the clip.

Different Perspectives

Write from multiple perspectives. Step out of your mind and view the world from someone else's perspective. Consider for instance how different people from different backgrounds might view the world. What are their views? Their struggle? Their ideas of what is right and wrong? What would they react to if placed in your circumstance? How would they respond differently to the challenges you have to overcome? Are they likely to make different choices from you?

Thinking about these and other questions can stimulate your brain and allow you develop new ideas and perspectives that might not have occurred to you in the first place.

Problem Solution

Everybody has issues however, most people don't take the time to sit and try to find solutions for our issues. That's the reason why journaling is so important. When you write down your issues, you'll gain a better understanding of the issue that is affecting you, the way it affects your life and the best way to solve the issue.

Journal Prompts

Utilize journal prompts and self-directed questions to guide you in writing. Journal prompts of good quality can prompt deeper self-research and can often reveal insights regarding yourself and your personal life which you may not have considered otherwise. Some simple examples include:

* What is your most-loved movie, book, or song or color, location or food item and what is the reason behind it?

• Do you have siblings? What are the similarities and the differences between you?

How do you know the commonalities and differences that you share with your peers?

* What do you enjoy doing and the reason for it?

What are your thoughts on your own society?

* If you had the chance change anything, what are the things you'd like to change in the world? What would you do?

Write about your ideal woman, man house, job or.

If you were to win the lottery What would you do with the winnings?

* If you're given the an opportunity to travel to any country that you would like to then which country would you select and why?

• Which novel, TV programor film has had a profound impact in your personal life?

Common Problems and Questions

1. I don't have time to write because I'm busy in my life of family and work, how should I be doing?

If you're reading this book, then you must be taking the idea of creating a journal seriously. Set it as a priority in your daily life and you'll be able to be able to find time. As mentioned earlier there are many ways to journal Some of them were designed specifically for those who are less productive. Keep in mind that you don't have to adhere to any of the ways of journaling discussed here. create a journaling routine that is based on your particular situation. All you really require is five minutes per day.

2. Where should I write?

Ideally, you'll need to locate an area that is peaceful and uncluttered. You should ensure that you feel at ease. The most important thing is to be at ease and capable of concentrating. Make sure you write at the same spot each day, if possible in order to develop a habit. The study area or office is perfect, provided they are available to you.

3. What happens if I'm constantly distracted and I can't seem to get for myself?

You can journal before going to bed or shortly when you get up to keep yourself away from other people. If you are in a room with others let them know that you are journaling at a certain time. They will eventually accept it.

4. I'm not a fan of the work I'm writing. how do I overcome this?

Remember that journaling is only for you and no anyone else than you. It requires practice to allow yourself to write in a way that is authentic. Try freewriting in order to remove self-imposed limits.

5. I'm concerned about the possibility of someone reviewing my journal. What can I do to overcome this issue?

Place your notebook in a secure location where no one else is likely to be looking. The safest place to store your journals is via a device that is digital Consider this as an option if you're extremely concerned about this matter.

6. What is the best frequency to write?

It is largely dependent on your personal preferences and the type of journaling style you prefer. The author suggests every day at least once for most people to ensure that the habit is maintained. It is important to have an established routine.

7. Do I need to know how long devote to in my journal?

This is dependent on the amount of time you can spare and what kind of journaling style you prefer. If you are doing meditative or reflective journaling take your time to develop your thoughts. However, don't do it too much, and journaling shouldn't become an exercise. Set a timer so that you can be sure that you adhere to the set amount of time. This helps to reduce procrastination as well as over-thinking.

8. There are many ways of journaling. I'm overwhelmed and I not sure which method to choose.

It's not worth thinking about you're overthinking it. Choose a form of journaling that you think is intriguing or helpful and go along. You are able to experiment and try new types of journals as you move on your journaling experience.

9. What happens if I'm more conscious of the things I write down because I believe my journal is very valuable?

It's normal to feel this way writing in your gorgeous notebook. Perhaps you'd like to only write about the thoughts and feelings that are worthy of being written down, and you revise what you write.

However, this doesn't meet the aim of keeping journals. You're not able to express your real feelings or the thoughts that lurk within your mind.

So, it's more beneficial to use a basic pen and paper, and allow yourself the liberty to air out your frustrations and, if you make mistakes, write everything in capital letters or simply cross out any words.

10. Do I have to keep several journals simultaneously?

There are journals that can be separate for various objectives. For instance, you could keep a gratitude journal, travel journal, or quote journals. This allows you to make use of your journals for specific topics and to write in a structured way. Additionally, they will become easier to reference them and locate the information you're looking for.

11. Are there any differences between diaries and journals?

Most often, diaries and journals are thought to be one in the identical. They are both cathartic and beneficial. But, there's one slight distinction between the two. The majority of people use journals to record what's happened. Journals are used to record their feelings about the events that have occurred, and what they anticipate to happen in the future. Journals allow them to look back on their experiences and then process them similar to what they would do with a counselor or a friend.

12. Writing a journal with hand more effective than using a telephone or computer?

In reality, journaling is beneficial regardless of the methods you employ. A handwritten journal comes with some advantages. First, it can slow you down. It is possible to type quickly and think quickly. When you write, however, you take your time and you have enough time to contemplate the content you write.

Furthermore, your handwriting may be influenced by the mood that you feel during that moment. Handwriting can provide lots of information about your mental state and mood. The way you write or how long your letters appear, if you cross out the t's and mark the i's, make mistakes in spelling or make other mistakes and then cross out words, all signify the state of mind. They reveal how you felt, whether you were angry or calm and composed when you wrote. All of these details could be missed if using computers or phones to write on.

13. Which is your most crucial thing you'd recommend to journal?

Write down what you are thinking or thinking or. Be honest. Journaling should be conducted in a the most unfettered manner with no editing.

14. What can you do when I have a notebook that is full?

It is contingent on the sentimental value it holds for you. A lot of people want to save the entirety of their journals as they have a connection to them. Some people take out pages that hold great memories or thoughts, and also the photographs or images that they like and reuse the rest of their notebook.

If the old journals you have can be a source of motivation in your life, it might be beneficial to keep them in your possession and use them when you require some direction or inspiration. However, if they're making you feel weighed down with old memories that hinder you from making progress it is best to eliminate them.

Chapter 5: Building The Habit

Once you're well-versed in the fundamentals of journaling, it's time to incorporate it into your routine and start to establish a habit of keeping a journal.

The steps to take to establish the habit are:

1. Commit

The first thing you must do is make the commitment to pick the plunge into journaling. You must be 100% committed to this practice within your head. This is vital since it is believed that if you have will, there's an opportunity. The rate at which a new habit develops is contingent on how much you are gung-ho about your new resolution.

Start by setting a date of 30 days, and commit to journaling during this period. Be honest and full of enthusiasm. Don't allow yourself to abandon the habit for even one day in the beginning stages. Don't make excuses to not write.

2. Share the information with others.

Let others know what you're planning to do as social pressure makes you accountable. When you inform others that you're adopting the habit of writing down your thoughts, you'll be amazed to find out how well you adhere to it. This is due to the fact that people tend to be more focused as well-organized when they are aware that others are watching to see whether they are able to keep their commitments.

If you know someone in your family who writes, consider creating a journaling friend'. A person who does exactly the same thing can help you stay accountable.

3. Create a Schedule

To be able to do the process in a regular method and develop an established routine, plan a specific time to do journaling. It is possible to reserve some time at the beginning of the day as your mind is fresh and open. Start your day with an inspirational thoughts. You can also write in your thoughts before you go to go to bed. This could be the perfect moment to let go of the burdens of the stress of a long day. You can let all the thoughts and feelings and rest peacefully. If you prefer, you can do it any time that is convenient for you throughout the day.

The time of day doesn't have much impact, but it is essential to keep it in the same time each day.

4. Start Simple

Try to make the process as easy as you can. Pick only one method for journaling at first. If it seems effortless you'll have more success sticking to the process. If the process gets too difficult it is possible to get frustrated and quit.

In addition, you'll be able master this method and then be encouraged to experiment with other methods.

5. Start Small

Journaling is a time-consuming activity. at first, but gradually increase the amount of time. If you set aside a huge chunk of time at first it could prove difficult to complete or you may get bored. If you can do it for just only a few minutes each day can make it more interesting and enjoyable. If you begin to enjoy it then you can increase your amount of time slowly. It will make sure that the practice lasts for a long duration.

6. Make sure you build this one Habit

When you begin writing make it a routine. Avoid introducing any other new routines simultaneously. Visualize and imagine that you are a prolific journalist. If you practice this habit regularly, your subconscious will be able to accept this new habit while the practice will also be strengthened.

Create an affirmative affirmation about journaling as a habit and repeat it to yourself repeatedly and over and again. This will assist you in get into the habit faster.

Keep going until your journaling routine becomes a part of your daily routine and you find it difficult to do it if absent.

7. Habit of stacking

Combine this new habit with an existing one. For example, if, for instance, you're accustomed to drinking coffee every morning, you can combine it with your new habit of writing. This can be extremely beneficial since the new routine is aided by the existing one.

8. Reward Yourself

It is important to reward yourself for your success in writing every day. It doesn't matter what you do, as long as it's tiny to be rewarded. The principle behind this is that whenever you reward yourself it reinforces and reinforces the behaviour. On the unconscious level, you begin to associate the pleasure in receiving an award this particular behavior. Thus, you'll realize that journaling is beneficial and you will begin planning to engage in this type of activity.

9. Experiment

Once the habit begins to develop, you can begin to become more adventurous. Explore different ways to find what works for you Explore different locations, time and formats of journaling.

For instance, you could mix different kinds of journaling, such as mincfulness journaling, reflective journaling or bullet journaling. You can also combine various methods of journaling like gratitude or creative and fitness, dream projects, reading one-sentence journals and morning page.

You can try journaling in different locations. You can, for instance, visit a park to look around at people and things from a distance. You can then write down your thoughts. You can also write down your observations while you travel by train. Try this in early morning hours morning or at various time of the day, and determine which is the most appropriate timing for you.

Chapter 6: How Should Record When You

Journal

It is recommended to write an outline of the content of your journal. This could be an opportunity for a group discussion and your daily routine or even your lab activities. Then, you can think about these activities , and then make notes of your thoughts or reactions to the activities you have recorded. Do your best to make notes about any doubts or confusions which may arise out of the exercises. As much as you can to utilize your journal to research different solutions to your issues or questions and then note the new knowledge that you discover through your strategies for problem solving. It is essential to be original and critical , or constructive, when writing.

How do I write a journal?

There isn't a single rules for journaling however, you must ensure that you write with ease and keep your thoughts as clear as you can. Based on the subject which you're journaling in it is essential to ensure that your writing is creative and thought-provoking. If you're engaging within Academic journaling, you have ensure that your thoughts are accurate and scientifically based. It is essential to provide accurate references to every lesson and concepts. If you're writing a journal for academic purposes it is essential to consider the aspects which piqued your curiosity or got you feel enthusiastic about the subject. Also, you should think about various ideas that could be developed from your past and present experiences.

The fundamentals of reflective journaling.

Simply stated, reflective journaling lets you think critically, specifically on the things people say and what you read , and the events that occurred. The process of reflection through thinking journaling requires four procedures that are

4. Justification of actions Find solutions, meanings, and make changes.

Stage 3 - Create assumptions, and discover the attributes as well as values and beliefs.

Stage 2 - Recall your experience.

1. Stage 1: Journaling.

The reflective thinking

Reflective thinking can be described as your own personal reaction to various situations, experiences or events, as well as new information. It is a process of journaling that brings the most effective aspects of your thinking and learn. There is no correct or wrong method for reflective thinking. You simply have to ask lots of questions.

When you consider the stages of reflective thinking described above, you'll discern that the process begins with your own thoughts. When you are beginning to think about the actions and words of others, you have to stop and take a look at your own thoughts, and that is to review your previous experiences with the topic you're writing about. It is also important to think about the reasons behind why and how you're thinking in the manner you do. Start by reviewing your own personal beliefs, thoughts and assumptions since they can influence how you think critically and reflective thinking. Therefore your attitudes, beliefs, and values form the basis of your understanding of journaling.

Reflective thinking in journaling demands you to bring your useful knowledge to every event that you encounter. Reflective thinking helps you to clarify your thoughts and draw attention to the essential connections between your knowledge and what is taking place in the world around you. Reflective thinking can help you get more involved when you journal and will assist you in becoming an active learner with a keen awareness of what's happening around him.

The benefits of reflective writing journaling?

Reflective writing is described as your reaction to new events, experiences and your own opinions. It could also be described to be a reaction to your personal thoughts and feelings. Journaling with reflection is advantageous because it allows you discover what you have learned and provides you with the opportunity to improve your knowledge about yourself. It's the best way to get clarity and greater understanding of the matter or subject you're studying as a journalist.

Reflective writing can help you improve and strengthen your writing abilities. It can help you make an explanation from the material you're learning or thinking about. Reflective writing isn't a method of expressing information or argument. It is distinct from mere descriptions, even although it does contain descriptive elements. You're not engaged in reflective journaling when you are making a simple judgement or take a decision about something, and it's not an easy problem-solving journaling tool. Journaling reflectively isn't an easy notepad or an essay, but it's a part of journaling where you critically evaluate the entire spectrum of points in favor and against the subject.

Why should you take a stand in your journaling?

There are four primary reasons to be a critical thinker when journaling

To connect your thoughts,

To critically evaluate your learning process

For clarification on the subject you are studying,

Reflect about your accomplishments and failures.

Connecting your journaling thoughtsThe principle for reflection is that the information you have learned previously must provide some prior knowledge or insight into the subject you are writing about. Whatever knowledge you've gained is informal or formal and reflective thinking can aid you in making connections between your knowledge and what you're currently learning. Reflective thinking helps you make connections between the two and also aids in connecting the things you're doing to the reason and why you're doing it.

Analyze or review your journaling process. This is a part of critical thinking which helps you to write reflective essays that help you reflect and comment on your experiences when you learn. It can help you evaluate what you've already learned and the reason for it.

Critical thinking can help you to make clearer understandings of what you are learning. Through reflective writing and thought you are able to simply provide clarifications about the fundamentals of the subject you've studied. Thinking and writing reflectively will assist you in integrating what already know and what you're learning, or have yet to discover.

Critical thinking will allow you to think about your successes and failures. Retrospectively examining your mistakes is one the most effective ways to making sure that you don't repeat the same mistakes reflections. Likewise, reflecting upon your previous successes can aid in identifying the basic concepts you can use to journaling time and repeatedly.

Writing and thinking critically can help you become an active learner and reflective practice.

How do you use an reflective style of writing in journaling

For those who are just beginning it is essential to begin doing the act of reflecting as quickly as is feasible. Reflective writing is a subjective process in the sense that it focuses on your thoughts. Therefore, your writing style has to be reflective and logical in the sense that it is reflective in. There is no one standard for reflective writing. you are able to write in any way that is personal, hypothetical, or critical. Nevertheless, you can make your writing based on your own experience however, don't limit yourself to your educational background.

Tips 1: You have to be aware that Reflective writing must contain the details (what is, when, and who are involved). Also, it must include an the analysis (how and what to do if). Reflective writing must be viewed to be an exploration tool that can bring more questions and answers.

Tip 2: While engaging in a reflective journaling activity it is possible to use a variety of styles of writing, which include the following:

Make it descriptive (Outline the things you'd like to record or the way you did something).

- Explain it (Explain the reasons why it happened or explain how it happened in the manner this).

Make it more explicit (I believe ...., I'm convinced). ....).

Tip 3. Make sure to make use of complete paragraphs as well with complete sentences when you write descriptive writing.

Tip 4: You are permitted to use personal pronouns, such as"I"and"my".

Tip 5: Use more informal words and phrases like as"Bloke"and"Kid".

How do you write reflectively?

- Before you begin writing your reflection, consider the following question: what topics can I write about?

Think about your impression of the subject matter and the material of the course.

Discuss your thoughts and experiences with your observations, and discuss how them be related to the subject you're journaling about.

You could also write about the elements you find challenging, challenging or difficult. You can also write about why you believe the elements have been described as such.

You are able to write about the ideas you've generated as well as the conclusions that you've made from the observations you have taken.

Write about the way you were successful in solving a problem by finding a solution, or come in a way that you can comprehend the subject.

You could also write about the potential results of your study or on the hypothesis you have drawn or your speculations.

You may write about the different interpretations you came up with or alternative perspectives you could have uncovered during the course of your study.

Write about the connections and similarities between the information you have gathered and the previous knowledge you had about the subject or between the information you have as well as the assumptions you've made. You could also write about the issues you must investigate through your thinking and actions, and also how the new concepts you've developed have challenged your previous knowledge or knowledge.

Beginning as a novice in journal writing

As a newbie it is recommended to follow these steps for journaling These steps will allow you to remain organized and write perfectly without making any mistakes.

Step 1: Give clarification regarding your tasks

An assignment for reflective journaling may take many forms, but they all require that you understand your assignment. Be sure to clarify any your doubts or questions about the topic.

Step 2: Give clarifications about the components of your practical

It is possible to incorporate images or media clips, when you describe the practical or physical elements of your descriptions. Hence you should make provision for these parts.

Step 3: Collect all your thoughts

This is among the longest-running aspects of writing a reflective journal. Before you begin writing, you should be able to critically think and think about what you intend to write on. Start the process of gathering your thoughts by creating a mind map. This can help to expand your mind as well as aid in organizing your thoughts prior to making different connections between your ideas and thoughts. Mind maps can aid you in organizing or structuring your thoughts.

To gather your thoughts efficiently You should take into consideration the following:

Inscribe the subject of the investigation in the middle of the blank page.

Draw all the related concepts or subjects using branches where different ideas are linked to the primary topic at the center. The branches should include any theories, authors and other experiences that relate to the primary subject. When a fresh idea arises, you just have to start a new branch from the middle.

To maintain your thoughts in a flow and to ensure that you don't lose any thought, you should organize your thoughts quickly. Be sure to associate with your ideas in a fluid manner and don't need to alter your ideas in this point.

Create a circle around the principal idea or point, then take an in-depth look at each thing on your drawing and observe how they relate to one another as well as the primary topic at the center.

Utilize arrows, lines and colors to establish an association between concepts and ideas. Also, you can make use of words and phrases to accomplish this.

A few suggestions that will assist you with reflective journaling

Try as many times as you can to imagine an event or interaction from your previous experience that could be relevant to the subject you are currently writing about.

Tell us about the events that occurred in your experience and the role you played as well as your feelings and thoughts that were triggered by the incident.

Consider what you can say about the situation to someone else and also what the lessons you have gained will are in relation to the scenario you're researching.

Consider different perspectives, theories and concepts you could apply to the current situation.

How to organize your journal entries

After you've gathered your ideas and thoughts You should think about how well you could connect your notes in order to organize them better;

Tips 1. Write an explanation or description of the process used in writing

Tip 2: Try as hard as you can to include any particular language or concept that is specific to your discipline (you have to write the explanation of the words at the bottom of your write-up).

Tips 3: Perform an evaluation of your methods you are using during your research.

Tip 4: Make the conclusions and recommendations you make basing your conclusions on your evaluations of all scenarios , not only your own personal experiences.

Notes from field work are useful when you write as a journalist. Jotting notes, for instance, can quickly help you remember specific details. It is recommended to consider taking notes on observation beneficial, particularly when you write in code. Keep an extra note that explains every abbreviation and code to make re-reading more straightforward for you.

Journaling rules that work for you to keep a journal.

If you wish making journaling as simple as you can, there are a some rules that you must be adhering to;

Rule number one: Work on a couple of pointers at one moment

There is no need to write a full sentence all at once. Just write a bullet points for the most important event that occurred in the course of a day (you could make up to 10 bullet point or even more). If you keep your day-to- journal entries brief and easy you can make an ideal journal later by expanding the bullet points you've created.

Rule 2: Store your notebook in a place where you won't be able to

Many journalists prefer keeping their notebooks near where they drink their morning coffee, while others prefer to store their notebooks in moleskins. It doesn't matter which nature of the notebook you are using for journaling. notebooks are perfect to journal in because you will get distracted by other things If you keep your journal in your laptop.

When you look at your notebook, you'll keep a note of when you journal. If you modify your routine for the day and begin having coffee somewhere else and you not remember to journal, which is why it is essential to keep your notebook near a routine is not likely to alter.

Rule #3: Do not miss the journaling for longer than

If you've missed more than two journals in a row, then you could need to devote a amount of time writing entries, and you'll have a difficult task of remembering what you've completed prior to. The presence of visitors could alter the routine of your life, so you could be required to search your calendar or emails to refresh your memory. You will also need to be sure to include a number of entries that you haven't added to your journal.

Keep in mind that it's always better to write down 24 hours after the incident has occurred, particularly when things are fresh in your mind. Although, it is possible to write after two days of an event , you'll miss important details and lose some aspects of the event when you decide to start journaling in three or more days. This is why it is essential to make sure that you don't skip more than two consecutive days without journaling.

Journaling for happiness and personal fulfillment (Tips and suggestions)

If you don't remember to write down your thoughts for a whole day or a few days then you may use your scheduler or emails to remind you of the things you have done.

Always be concise, and simply create bullet points of the most important things you accomplished like: 1. Thurs. March 13 15th, 2015. Exercise, week's end. 2. We received decorations and gifts for Mark and Chloe's wedding. 3 Drafted the final year's school project.

Do your best to start your journal in the morning, before you go to your computer. Do your best to review your day prior to. Be sure to avoid journaling on the computer. If you do, you could not remember to journal. Be sure to look at the past and look back on the highlights of the day. This can help you decide whether you've been focusing on the most important things instead of the ones that waste your time.

If you're a committed to being a journalist, you should be able to keep a journal on a regular basis as it can help you discover new avenues of opportunity which can spark your self-discovery abilities and self-expression. Sometimes it is possible to look at the wall in a blank space without anything to write about, and you might get so overwhelmed that you do not have any ideas to write about. If this is the case then you must think about the following:

Keep journaling easy and enjoyable.

When you begin to feel like journaling has turned into a chore, it's time to have breaks . If you like using fanciful art as journals then you could simply alter your the direction and keep a written journaling for a bit. If you are a regular journaler and it seems like your daily schedule isn't giving enough time, you could take a to rest between. You could consider journaling three or four days in a week , but it is essential to not spend more than 2 days without checking your journal . This will keep you on track.

Keep journaling fun

If you're not finding journaling to be enjoyable and satisfying activity, you'll be bored and will probably not have any new ideas to record about. If you're not able to come up with ideas, you might need to stop and try a different approach. If this is the case, you'll need to add more imagination to your journaling. You can make fun of journaling by adding some stickers to your journal There are a variety of amazing stickers you can put on backgrounds to enhance your journaling experience. It is possible to replace your normal marker with a magical one These little items could make you fall in the love of journaling once more.

Try as hard as you can to keep journaling as short as you can

Some people might not think of journaling for a shorter duration as a way to improve their journaling. Writing in short lengths can save time, and you won't become bored often. Making your journaling brief is the best choice you could consider when you're not sure you've got enough time, especially when you are still working and take care of other obligations. It is easy to utilize the timer in your phone or watch to take this approach.

When you set the timer to journal and you start to stick to the schedule and when the alarm starts you can simply finish your work and review the work you've accomplished to date. The timing will allow you the opportunity to finish your work in a steady manner and you won't need to be ed ting all at the same time.

The most enjoyable journals to keep

In addition to keeping a record cf your feelings, thoughts, and experiences, there's many different kinds of journals that you could think about, but bear your mind in the present that you do not have to keep a journal each day, so you might not be able to maintain more than one journal at an time. The most effective kinds of journals to keep are:

-Family journals. Writing down your personal life and family can be a lot of fun. Your children, parents and cousins, nephews, aunts and uncles will surely make a positive impact on your daily life. One of the most effective ways to make it fun is to host an evening of family journaling where the family can get together to discuss their journals. Make sure that they have illustrations to add enjoyable.

- Letter journal. If you are a fan of writing letters or keeping them then you should keep a copy for each letters in your binder file and make an album from the letters.

Memory journal - This kind of journal can assist you to recall everything that has occurred in the past. It can be an ideal companion for those who travel for long distances.

Prayer Journal - A prayer journals are great when you're spiritually inclined . It is easy to look back at your prayer journal and observe what prayers you were answered.

Journal of movies and books - If you are looking record your favorite books and movies, then you should keep a diary of these items. It is important to share your experiences particularly when you go to the movies with those you are passionate about.

The Couples Journal is the perfect method of bringing fun to your relationship or marriage. It gives you the opportunity to spend some time to write about your partner. It's even more enjoyable if your spouse also writes. Journal about your dreams for the future and the ways you'll achieve these dreams.

A journal for friendship is among the most beautiful journals you could consider because it allows you to keep those wonderful times you spent with your loved ones. Keep a record of the meal you shared with a friend who you haven't met before and the places you went to. An account of your friendship could be something you're hoping to get from an office co-staff position at the workplace you work in.

Birthday journals - This is the ideal method to record every person you've met n your thoughts. You can ask your friends to select their birthdays and then ask them to remind you of the time they first met you and why they are so passionate about you and record what you admire about them as well. By keeping a birthday journal you won't need to keep track of your calendars for birthdays, but this kind of journal requires regular revisions.

Do you enjoy cooking? Or do you like watching various cooking shows? Do you enjoy watching cooking shows on TV? Do you want to keep a record of your favorite cooking shows or keep a record of your old and current recipes. You must include the source of your recipes along with the location and when they were served. It is also possible to write down the opinions and emotions of those in attendance at the moment the food was served. Keep a journal of meals, lunches desserts, special events and recipes.

Journals of exercise or sports-whether you're actively involved in sports , or play for pleasure and healthreasons, you must keep a record of it. You can keep a record of your favorite sports team as well as your local sports club, whether it's a city or town club.

Diet Journals - a diet journal will help you track what you eat and also what you can improve your diet particularly when trying to lose some weight. Journals for weight can contain the types of exercises you perform and the distances have covered during your workout and the amount of repetitions that you performed and the general tracking the progress you make in exercising.

A finance journal is a great way to keep track of your monthly or daily expenses through keeping a journal of your finances. It is also possible to keep a record of family expenses and help maintain a track of your current financial situation. A financial journal can assist you in tracking what you intend to do to make changes regarding your spending.

Journal for your hobby-do you like traveling? Going to shows and events across the globe? Do you enjoy collecting things like coins, stamps and furniture? You should start keeping an account of your hobbies, it allows you to record your thoughts about your experiences, observations and people you have met during your pursuit of these hobbies.

Focus journal - One of the most effective methods to achieve your goals is to write down a diary of the things you've done over the years. The journal will help you reflect or do some critical review of what you've committed a mistake in the past, and how you can alter your circumstances or change it for the way you approach it to attain satisfaction and happiness for yourself. Keep a journal of your current focus and what you are focusing on towards the future. It can help you stick to an idea for the future.

Chapter 7: Strategies On How To Journal

Effectively

Journaling is not restricted to any specific group of people. If you're able to write, you can participate in it. In the above paragraph:

There are a few actions you can take to improve your journaling and improve your outlook and reap many benefits from it.

This chapter we will examine strategies that you can employ to establish a regular journaling routine throughout your day. For you to begin the first thing to do is:

#: Pick an appropriate medium

The first thing you need to do is select the journaling medium you want to use. The medium you choose can be:

Pen and notebook

Notebooks and pens are an old-fashioned method for journaling that remains extremely effective today. Penciling the words down on paper. If you record each word with your own handwriting, it's like writing your heart out into the work you're writing.

Find a quality notebook and a pen with a stylish design. You want something that brings your heart to consider writing inside it. Notebooks don't need to be expensive. If you're just beginning to journal it is recommended that a basic spiral notebook can start -- but it must be appealing. Then, you can buy a larger, more expensive journal to keep your notes in if you want to.

A smartphone app

There are many apps you can use to record notes, save images, and even record moments. It is possible to make use of these apps, especially those who are already typing on your smartphone.

For instance you can use the note feature on your phone might be an option you aren't using often and yet you are able to compose over a thousand sentences on it. It is also possible to use apps like Penzu to start your journaling.

The benefit of journaling using your phone is that you'll have easy internet access any time and consequently, use it to record some notes without being obvious. In addition, as with most people, you utilize your phone frequently so journaling on your phone isn't difficult.

Your computer

Laptops and personal computers can be useful when writing. You can utilize Scrivener as well as Microsoft Word to type in your thoughts, and then use a cloud-based software such as Dropbox as well as Google Drive-- to store your documents. So, you'll be able to access them after an event like a crash occurs on your PC.

It is important to note the fact that writing your thoughts on computers might not be an easy task to get used to or initially. You might find yourself stuck on the initial word, particularly if you do not use the computer often. But the more you work at it -- even in the event that you need to look at an empty screen for a few minutes-the more easy it will become.

In the end, regardless of what medium you decide to use the main aspect to keep in mind is that all you'll need is a place to write down the thoughts, concepts, feelings and so on.

Your journaling medium is an instrument. The way you use it will determine how effective you are in journaling.

Once you have chosen a journaling medium Next stage is:

#: Choose a location

Journaling can be done anywhere you like. However, it's best to select a specific place to journal. The presence of a particular journaling space will allow your brain to connect that location with journaling. So, when you are sitting down, your brain will go into "journaling mode" since that's what you've been taught to do.

Pick a spot that's peaceful, and preferably that is free of interruptions. Distractions can affect the flow of your writing.

#: Choose a topic

What will be the theme of your journaling sessions? Before you start you must answer.

If you're not sure of the subject to write about, you could begin by writing down the things which are bothering you. Write about an incident, an incident or disagreement with an individual. Begin by identifying the incident and then write about it within your diary as fully as you are able to.

Then, you should write how the event caused you to feel and how it connects your relationships. Let yourself express your feelings on paper. Allowing things to flow naturally allows you to journal freely and more enjoyable.

Do not stop at describing your experience and feelings.

Think about what you could have done differently, and what you'd do differently should the same situation occurs again. When you attempt to do this, keep in mind the fact that writing is an ongoing procedure.

Nobody expects you to know all the answers. And the answers you be able to answer right now could change in a few days or months from the present. The most important thing is to note down where you are at the moment. It's likely that you'll revisit the subject in the future.

When you're using journaling to address your past experiences, you have be aware of the way you feel. If it becomes difficult to write about your feelings write about it, put it aside or simply write about how you're feeling and not write further. You can continue to write about other subjects until you are competent to write about your previous traumas without feeling overwhelmed.

Another thing to think about is:

The length and frequency

If you begin journaling, write for between 15 and 20 minutes, at a minimum, for one week. Write every day and never quit until the time you've set is set. If you don't wish to think about your clock setting an alarm or a timer could be very useful.

If you don't have anything to say, you could write it again or even paraphrase it. It's also possible to write about having nothing to write about.

It may sound odd, but the practice requires writing, which is the thing you should do until you are more comfortable writing. When you share your challenges, you might spark other thoughts and then begin writing about them.

How long should you write? How much do you need to write?

If you consider it, you'll realize that certain thoughts are simple to express in a couple of words, while you need more to think about other possibilities. Don't worry over the amount of words you've written. But, do your best to get deep into those thoughts. If you can do that you'll be writing more often, but not feeling like you've done too many.

#: Only write for yourself

When you're journaling the general rule is to write to yourself. It's not about recording things that occurred. You're exploring them and understanding how they impact your behavior and feelings.

In order to achieve this you must:

* Be truthful: Personal honesty is something that you cannot escape by writing only for yourself. Journals let you look into difficult topics. It allows you to look at yourself with a critical eye and ask yourself all the questions you're not comfortable asking anyone other person. With honesty, you'll arrive at certain conclusions and improve as an individual.

Keep it confidential A reason you might not want to write down your personal thoughts is because you are afraid of that someone else might get a access to your journal and making use of your journal against you. If that's the case you should make sure that you keep your journal secure especially when you share your home with others. If you're required to take the steps, you can purchase the box and key and keep your journal locked inside. If you're wired to computers or phones it's possible to secure your passwords for phone, files or computers.

Do not be a perfectionist: Journaling is not the moment to be concerned about spelling or grammar mistakes. It's a personal journal while you may be strict with things such as grammar, it's essential to keep in mind that you're writing down the thoughts of your mind not polished thoughts. By adopting this approach, you'll have the ability to write down ideas without focusing on grammar. You can create sentences, words, phrases or draw things. Give yourself the freecom to express yourself freely without being concerned over grammar guidelines.

Concentrate your attention When you're writing, you must focus your concentration on what you're writing. That means you need to shut off your television and switch off your mobile and avoid engaging in conversation with your other friends. When you have set aside time for journaling, you should block out all other activities until you've completed the journal.

Your writing style is unique to what you write when are aware that other people will read your writing. There are no rules that apply, aside from the ones you would like to adhere to. Don't be afraid to experiment rather than trying to make journaling be something you can imagine allow your writing to flow and let it guide you.

If you're hesitant to write your thoughts down and write them down, you could ruin the work you've written once it's done. With this "safety net" will permit you to express your most intimate thoughts without reserving them or worry about being exposed.

#: Make sure you remember the specifics

Specifics are crucial to writing. The human brain tends to lose many details in the course of time. This is the reason you should note down all the information.

Once you begin writing, make a note of the date you started writing. When you recall events, aside from jotting down your thoughts it is also important to noting the place and the date the incident occurred, and the individuals who were involved.

Be aware that the little things that are on the forefront of your thoughts at the moment won't remain fresh in your mind. With time, you'll start to forget things, especially when emotions ease. Noting down the details will aid you in the future when you recall the incident.

#: Experiment with different perspect ves

You can enhance your journaling skills by trying different methods of writing. You can:

Upload photos

Pictures convey more than words could ever. This is because they record moments and draw the attention of things you could overlook. So, adding pictures will improve the journaling process.

An image may also encourage writers to think about different items. Through studying the image it can give you fresh ideas. For instance, you could be able to discuss the person in the image and who was in the picture, what the situation was or any other aspect associated with that particular moment. Since you'll be giving an "long description," you won't feel like you're trying to locate the right words.

Tell an interesting story

The great thing about telling an account is that actual experiences can be the inspiration however, you have the creative freedom to modify the story in any way you want. Imagine a specific memory , and then turn it into an engaging story. Childhood memories are great for stories.

For instance, you could transform a story you have of you or your family members being jolly into a tale complete with a moral edification. In this way, you can preserve the memory and add the story in a positive light which makes you remember the experience with fondness.

Your stories don't need to be adorable.

If you're having a problem with a friend or neighbor, you could create a an account of the issue. This will allow you to reduce tension, without increasing the issue. Storybooks can aid you in learning to view things from a new perspective. When you consider the characters and begin to develop the characters, you'll discover some things about the subject and may find yourself seeing things in a different way.

Write letters

The art of writing letters is something that we must not ignore. When you write an address to a person you love it's as if you're writing about your feelings and telling the person the way you feel or how you truly feel.

If you are interested in journaling journals, they can be your best friend. It is possible to use the letter-form format to write on it and write down your thoughts and feelings to the max. Start your writing with a 'Dear Diary', and then write as if writing to someone else about something important to you.

The benefit of writing this method is that it permits you to create a kind of organization. It allows you to discuss issues that you would normally not discuss in a journal. within your journals.

If, for instance, you're discussing someone, you'll need to identify the person in a way that the person you call a friend knows the person you're speaking about. In this way, it will seem like you're contemplating the person, rather than focus on the things he or did.

Another thing you could do is compose a letter to your former self or to your future self. The letters typically include information like learnings or words of encouragement.

For instance, if you feel that your younger self was having trouble following a certain route or navigating some particular issue You can write to your self-prepared self reminding yourself that in the end everything will be okay. This will bring comfort to the part of you which was hurt as a child. You'll see that even though you were hurt through it, you learned and improved in the process.

Free Write

Freewriting involves writing down whatever comes to mind. This is writing without any motivation or structure, nor direction. The concept is to take out your pen and notebook and begin writing whatever thoughts pop into your head. It could be a sentence or an idea, a thought or anything else. Your writing doesn't need to be perfect or cohesive.

In order to begin freewriting You can set up an alarm clock and choose how long you'll be spending in freewriting. For instance, you could choose to write over 15 minutes. That's right, you'll note down anything you think of during fifteen minutes or until the alarm sounds.

Use personification

There are many objects, both inanimate and animated, around you that could create great stories if they were given the chance to tell their stories. Personification can be used to give them the ability to speak. When you make use of personification, you will learn to view things from a different viewpoint.

Use a journaling prompt

These days, many writers are using prompts to add some flair in their work. Prompts can be something you make use of when journaling. They can aid you in thinking about what's going on within your daily life.

A few examples of prompts are:

* Your dream vacation

* The effect your favorite film will have on you

* If you happened to meet a ghost,

* If you were _

What would you do if you were

The concept is to use the prompt to get you started with your writing. It is possible to go even further and decide the number of words you'll use. For instance, you could write about your dream holiday with 250 words. In this way, you'll avoid from offering one-sentence responses.

Overall the writing process from different angles can enhance your journaling experience as it lets you discover many different things.

#: Don't stress

Most importantly, you should not worry about journaling. Journaling is about exploration. Through time you'll improve in not just writing your thoughts, but also in recognizing your thinking pattern.

Journaling can help you change your thinking and attitude However, change doesn't occur over night. It starts with the smallest of things. So, if you're able to only write just a few sentences at one time, then take the time to write however, try to write frequently. Once you have established your own journaling routine it will become more easy to write and analyze your thoughts in greater depth.

After having discussed how you can begin a successful journaling regimen, let's look at the advantages of journaling in your daily mental health, your life and clarity:

The Health, Life, and the benefits of writing

We've reviewed the best practices and techniques you can apply to begin a productive journaling routine.

While you've now got the knowledge, however you'll find it difficult to be committed to something when you're not certain what will happen to your life.

Journaling can be a great way to have enjoyment However, there are additional advantages to journaling. This chapter we'll examine the advantages of journaling on different aspects of your lives starting with life journaling:

The life-changing benefits of journaling

The act of writing down your experiences, thoughts and thoughts about life helps you maintain your identity create yourself into the person you'd like to be and establish your own identity. Consider this:

Every person has ambitions in our lives. But, more often than not the person you wish to be might not be who you currently are.

For instance, you might have written down your goals a few years ago, and hoped to achieve them. However, as time progress, you might be in the same position with the same goals, and still hoping to reach the identical goals.

It is a fact that wishing to do something isn't the same thing as actually taking action. It is more than simply dream about something. You must take action to turn your dream into become a reality. Journaling can aid you in this.

Writing about your life can help you:

#: Keep track of your progress towards your objectives.

Journaling is a procedure. Its goal is to motivate you to continue working on a problem until you have the solution. It's not a simple matter of saying you want something and then letting it be in that state. Journaling can help you to write down your progress toward the goals you have set.

You might, for instance, think that your schedule is too busy, especially during the mornings. Journaling requires you to look at the factors that can make your life stressful and come up with ways to make your life easier.

In this scenario you can make a decision to develop an evening routine to simplify your life early in the morning. It is possible to organize your clothing, pack bags, then then prepare for the following day at night.

The actions you choose to accomplish and your progress towards accomplishing them will be should be -- a permanent record in your journal. Also, you'll record the ways in which they have benefited your life. So, the positive outcomes you discover will demonstrate the benefits of making changes that will bring happiness into your life. It will also inspire you to take small steps toward your goals.

#: It improves your physical health

As you are aware that your health is a top priority. Many people, unfortunately, tend to ignore warning signs and signs the body exhibits when something isn't functioning properly.

If you keep a journal of your day-to-day life, one of the things you'll write about is your feelings. This means that if you suffer from an stomachache, headache or toothache, a backache, or feel nauseated or dizzy and nauseated, you'll be writing these symptoms down.

Let's get this straight. It's easy to dismiss symptoms that go away within a short period of time. If, however, those symptoms return or you are experiencing a range kinds of signs, it's likely that you'll begin being more aware of the way you feel.

Journaling can help you identify patterns. For instance, you might be feeling gassy after eating a specific dish or food. So, you could decide to remove that food from your diet in order you can improve the overall health of your body. Small changes that you make can add up to improve your health. If you're having issues with your fitness, keeping a journal will help you keep track of what you do with your time and how you're progressing to improve your fitness levels.

If you're looking to improve your health, you need to identify where the challenges within your life originate. Journaling can help you identify that. When you are aware that you are aware, you can take the necessary actions to address your problems to live more happily.

#: It helps improve your relationships

One of the benefits of journaling is that it can allow you to explore your relationships. According to a research study done by Stanford University, when you write you are more likely to concentrate on positive outcomes, even when confronted with difficult situations. This, in turn helps reduce your stress and gives you an optimistic outlook on your life.

Human beings tend to put emphasis on negative aspects even though there are many positive happenings within our daily lives. If you're used to certain people you could begin to take these people as a given. You might begin to ignore the positive aspects of them and begin to focus on all the negative things they do. Journaling can help you focus your thoughts and help you appreciate the small things in life.

Journaling about your life can help you record those moments that make life as it should be. It lets you know the state you're in with respect the goals you have set, strengthens relationships, and aids you make the changes you're capable of changing in order to improve your life. It also assists you in integrating your experiences from life and the lessons you've learned for your future interactions.

Now let's take a look at the mental health benefits of journaling

Journaling for Mental Health Benefits Mental Health Benefits of Journaling

According to a research study conducted by Cambridge University, journaling can enhance wellbeing following trauma or stressful experiences.

In the course of their study, researchers requested participants to spend 15 minutes to record their incidents. Results showed that they saw improvements in their physical and mental health.

Journaling can provide many mental health advantages for the mind:

* Enhances your focus

* Aids in processing emotions.

* Remains focused and as a result you'll have the ability to modify them or incorporate them

* Helps you release feelings that are bottled up and to discover thoughts that aren't fully formed.

* Helps you gain a better understanding of your thinking and actions

* Frees up the thoughts of your mind and concepts, and lets you let go of the memories from the past.

It connects your internal thoughts with your actions and external situations. It helps you understand the impact of your thoughts on your actions

* It allows you to look back at your life in the adult's perspective and,

* It helps to maintain stability, as it helps to reduce mental disarray.

Rememberthat your mental health can be affected by the circumstances that are happening in your daily life. Journaling can help you identify the things that make you feel happy as well as the things that cause your grief. It helps you see the things that you believe are vital in your life. This lets you concentrate on them instead of being surrounded by negative thoughts.

How Journaling Helps Improve Clarity

One of the primary reasons why people keep journals is to gain clarity. Journaling can help you dig deeper into thoughts, feelings and actions. It lets you be honest about the things that drive you. When you record your thoughts on clarity, you concentrate on:

* Facts

* Times

* Participants

* Feelings

* Thoughts

* Biases and

* Conclusions

So you'll be able look at things as they are and not how you would like they would be. As you've probably guessed, emotions can cloud situations and events. When this occurs, you might feel overwhelmed or trapped in your past instead of finding an avenue ahead.

Journaling to help you be clearer helps you:

#: Problem-solve

Journaling allows you to see connections. It's about wholeness rather than separation. This is the key:

When you're overwhelmed by a situation it's easy to make unwise decisions or get angry. Journaling can help you slow down so that you can look at the issue in all its aspects and allow you to look at the issue and determine the most effective solution.

#: Be aware of yourself better

Journaling can help you dig deeply into who you are as an individual. Once you've gotten used to it, you'll come to understand your beliefs as well as your thoughts, behaviors, your feelings and beliefs.

While you're writing and examining yourself, you're using an incredibly fine-tooth comb. It allows you to remove the mask and look at yourself not as the person you'd like to be instead, as you are now. Understanding what your weaknesses and strengths are can help you make better choices regarding your daily life, particularly when it comes to having to deal with other people.

#: Heal

Writing with clarity and clarity in your life allows you to repair your relationships as in healing previous wounds. It assists you in determining what's bothering you and the reason it's troubling you. It helps you pinpoint what's bothering you rather than putting the label of your feelings. For instance, instead of telling a story that causes you to feel bad or 'unpleasant,' you could say it makes you feel'sad or angry.'

After you have labeled your emotions You can then begin to determine the reason these feelings occur. What is the reason you are feeling sad? What is the reason you are feeling angry? The answers you can come up with will help you figure out what's going on and what steps you should make to be happier.

Rememberthat as you write about life, mental health and clarity, you must to reflect on the words you've written. Meditation is a major aspect of journaling. It is important to review the notes you've written down. This helps you look at things from a fresh perspective after your brain has had time to reconcile the ideas and bring your thoughts in line.

Journaling can change your outlook which is why it such a powerful instrument. Apart from allowing you to speak to yourself, it also allows you to develop as a person as it allows you to understand how your thoughts impact your actions and decisions. So, if you realize that what you're doing isn't working then you'll be able to alter your habits and this will result in a positive overall impact to your personal life.

In reality, the value of journaling isn't something that we can exaggerate about. Journaling is a good thing because it's a fundamental design. It's similar to having a personal psychologist or a highly trusted close friend. It's similar to having someone who's open, reliable honest, impartial, and non-judgmental standing by your side. A person like that is one who will listen to your concerns and allow you to be yourself and draw new conclusions.

So, don't be reluctant to give journaling a go because the benefits make it worth giving it a an attempt.

Let's get it straight:

Journaling helps you change your outlook and improve your life by helping you tackle the issues that arise in your life. It also helps by helping you see the possibilities that are available so that you can be successful regardless of the challenge you encounter.

How Journaling Can Help Change Your Perspective

There are two kinds of mental models:

The first is the fixed-mindset. This type of thinking believes that intelligence is not changing. If you are a fixed mentality that is based on fixed thinking, you are more likely to be in the habit to avoid challenges, and often giving up when you run into challenges, view that putting in effort and time as ineffective and ignore feedback from negative sources, and consider the accomplishments of others as a threat your own.

Also, a fixed mindset can limit the growth of your mind because it forces people to believe that there's no way to change the situation you're in.

The second kind of mindset is called the growth mindset

A person with a growth mindset believes that intelligence can be developed. In other words, if are in a state of growth, you can learn to take on the challenges that come your way, you persevere when faced with setbacks and view your effort as a means to master situations, you gain knowledge from your mistakes, and strive to gain insight from the achievements of others.

Journaling can help you develop a growth mindset and assists you in getting rid of the rigid mindset. It helps you to consider all ways you can develop the abilities necessary to excel in all areas of your life.

What kind of journals should you keep?

Chapter 8: Types Of Journals And

Advantages

There are a variety of types of journaling, each serving an individual purpose. Let's examine the primary types and their benefits:

Gratitude Journal

In the world of life, it's easy to be focused on negative things because they are able to stand out from a ocean of good things. The good things fade into background noise, just like the wall clock you've grown familiar with after having seen it repeatedly.

When something is negative you bring it to the forefront and focus on it which in turn makes you feel in a negative mood. It affects the way you conduct your day and how you interact with other people.

A gratitude journal is focused on the positive aspects of your life. It helps remind you that you have plenty of things to be grateful for. Things you could write into your grateful journal are:

• A listing of three to five things you are thankful for.

* Family member or friend who can provide support

* Hobbies that make you smile

* The time when a friend shocked you

* A nice memory

* Enjoying your favorite food

* Nature

A gratitude journal isn't only a list of good things or the blessings that you experience in your life. It's also a reminder of the fact that all is not lost. It allows you to escape the pressures of life. This means you'll be happier about yourself, admired by people around you, and have less stress.

Instead of tackling your day with fear as you write and reflect on your day, you'll have the ability to accept it with the knowledge that even though there are some negative aspects in the world but the positive aspects of life are more important. This shift in mental outlook will be apparent in the way you approach your day. Instead of viewing obstacles as obstacles that are meant to make you feel down, think of them as minor obstacles and obstacles you can get through while working toward your goals.

Being grateful helps you to see the small things, as well as the bigger things. Instead of focusing on major achievements, it makes you aware enough to be able to appreciate small wins, which inspires you to go on.

Food Journal

The food you consume affects the health of your body and mind and health. It affects your mental health, physical well-being and your energy levels. Therefore it makes sense to track what you eat. This is where a food diary is essential.

A food journal can help you keep track on your eating patterns. It should include information like your meals for the day as well as the type of food you consume, the amount you eat, as well as the time of your meals. It is also important to keep track of your feelings after eating certain food items. This way, you will find out if you suffer from food sensitivities.

It is also possible to use a food diary to:

* Lose weight: If you're looking to shed some weight, it is important to monitor the amount of food you consume, which can be difficult when you don't keep the record of your food intake. take in. A food journal can help to keep accurate record of your main meal and your snacks. People who keep a food journal when trying to shed weight will shed more weight than those who do not. This is because they are more conscious of the kind of food they're eating and the calories they consume, particularly when it comes to food.

• Embrace healthy eating Note down all the food that you consume will allow you to assess whether you're following the right diet. It can also help you monitor the changes you're making in order to cleanse your eating habits. Write about your experiences, the difficulties that you're confronting, and how these changes affect your. The positive effects you can see be a motivator to keep to your diet plan.

• Check the way you eat: A journal of your food can help you understand your eating patterns and habits. If you're struggling with poor eating habits, like eating food when you're stressed or eating food every time you watch TV your food journal will reveal these patterns. This will allow you to alter your habits.

A food diary can aid in introducing new food items in your life and diet. Instead of just eating the food you're familiar with, it may encourage you to make efforts to experiment with new recipes, and also discover food items and spices that you might enjoy. While you're at it you can experiment with various cuisines and discover various cultures.

Journals can help you discern certain facts, such as the changes you must make to reach your goals for health. The act of writing down your diet will make you aware of the things you put into your body and what effects it can have on your health and your life. This awareness will help you to make permanent significant changes that will aid you in making choices based on the facts and experience.

Workout Journal

It is something you can enjoy both psychological and physical advantages. If you're new to fitness You may end up confronting certain obstacles that could stop you from achieving your goals.

In the beginning, you could be prone to take on more than you are capable of and you might be tempted to compare yourself to others, or be disappointed when you don't see significant changes. A journal of your workout allows you to keep track of your workout and the progress you make.

It lets you see the effort you're making and the tiny changes the body as well as your mind experience. Rememberthat working out does not only mean changing your body into an unfathomably lean machine. It can also make you feel healthier and more energetic.

The scale might say that you've been losing weight however you could experience changes in your energy levels and measurements that indicate your progress. A fitness journal takes into consideration these changes and allows you to determine if your changes aid you in the bigger goals you have set for yourself.

The things you can put in your exercise journal include:

* Your progress each week Your weekly report must include details such as your measurements and weight. You can take measurements of your hips, chest, waist, legs, arms and waist. You can also upload photos so you can see your progression.

* Your thoughts: You must take note of your emotions and moods, as well as your thoughts, as well as any other issues you may face.

* Your workout program Choose which actions you'll engage in during your workout routine. For instance, you could do strength training, go for walks, or practice yoga. Make a workout routine that you are able to

complete and track your progress and modify your program as you get adept at the exercises.

* Your exercise method Once you have decided on your preferred exercise and workout it is important to be attentive to your method of training. In the beginning, you might not be able do certain exercises with ease however, as time goes along, your technique will improve. Keep track of the improvement on your notebook.

Flexibility is a component of your exercise routine. It lets you know the progress you've made , even the other measurements are still stationary. The ease at which you perform certain exercises could be a sign to you of the fact that you're now able to perform more intense exercise routines. This will boost your confidence in continuing your exercise routine.

Overall it is a journal that connects different aspects of your life. It reveals the impact of your exercise on your mood, your thinking as well as the way you look and feel. Being aware of this lets you make adjustments that improve your quality of life.

Reading Journal

You shouldn't overlook when looking to alter your lifestyle and your mindset. Books can provide you with knowledge. They expose you to diverse perspectives and challenge the way you think.

One thing you need to be aware of about books is that they:

Reading the books that you're reading hold the capacity to alter your perception. So, it's important to record the genres, authors of the book, the themes in the book as well as the characters and the way they interact with you, your impression of the book and how you would rate it.

In addition, note your book's title, as well as the date you began reading it, and also when you finished it. If you're looking to broaden your horizons do not limit yourself to the authors you've read. Consider reading books by other authors.

If you're experiencing difficult times self-help guides can assist you in getting back on your feet. An organized journal of reading will help you follow the tips you learn from these books. By doing this you'll do more than simply supplying yourself with knowledge. You'll improve your skills by engaging in a way that will bring about a significant change.

Certain books, like cookbooks on cooking or woodworking are able to help you master a particular skill. For instance, if you would like to learn bake, you can buy a few cookbooks that instruct you on what to do when baking. The knowledge gained from reading books will help you develop a more independent. As you improve your skills you'll be more confident in yourself and enhance your life by applying the skills you've learned.

Garden Journal

Gardening, similar to journaling can be therapeutic. It's a pastime that you can take part in to help you deal with the stresses within your daily life.

Once you've started your garden, you'll be able to write down the plants you're planning to plant, the date when you planted them, the many seedlings were planted and the fertilizer you used as well as the weather conditions and any other actions you take to take care of your plants and ensure they're strong and healthy.

You may also write down any observations that you may have about your garden. As time passes by you'll notice your accomplishments as well as learn lessons that you can apply to future gardening endeavors. When you look at the outcomes of your work and learn that you can appreciate your efforts.

Journaling is a great way to record the significance of gardening to you and to relate your experience to the rest of your life.

If you're planning to plant some vegetables, be sure to note the reasons you picked these plants and the benefits they provide for your body. Recording these things can help you understand food so that you'll be able to establish an appropriate relation to your food.

If you have children You can use this chance to educate them about the foods you plant as well as help you snap photos and draw images to include in an account of your gardening. This could be something you do with your family, not only to gain knowledge on plants but also to spend time with your family.

Pregnancy Journal

The effects of pregnancy affect not just the woman in the womb but the people who are around her.

Women who are pregnant go through many positive and negative shifts and emotions. However, the expectations of society can make you reluctant to voice your concerns and worries and that is why the pregnancy journal comes into.

A pregnancy journal is an closest companion as you go through the entire pregnancy process. It can be used to keep track of:

* Worries, emotions as well as ups and downs

* Unusual signs

• What food you consume, and the foods you hate or desire

* Any baby names you can come up with

* Watch your baby's movements

* Pictures of your baby's bump

Important dates and times

* The hospital visits you make

A pregnancy journal will remind you that you're an individual with needs to take care of, even when you are preparing for the birth of your child. It is a good way to keep track of what you're doing to look after yourself.

Another option to keep the pregnant journal would be to create an entertaining record of your experiences and mishaps. When you experience shifts and interactions with other and interact with others, you'll encounter circumstances that cause you to be awestruck, stunned or even embarrassment. It is possible to recount these incidents and add a humorous twist to the story. In this way you'll have the ability to release the negative feelings the event created, allowing you to take pleasure in your pregnancy, regardless of the bumps in the process.

When you look back on the time you had your baby, you'll smile and cry at the memories. It's also possible to discover things you've forgotten about particularly if you suffered from "pregnancy brain.'

Travel Journal

The experience of traveling to other countries as well as meeting new people and experiencing other styles of living will surely have a an impact on you. It can help you alter your perspective and appreciate the diversity. Travel journals will help you record your memories. In this way, you'll be able to be able to share them with friends later or simply enjoy recalling your travels and memories.

Don't delay your travels to begin a travel journal. Write it out prior to your trip.

Imagine your trip and the reasons you picked it, the locations you'd like to visit and what you expect from the journey. Record these thoughts along with your expectations for the trip and your journey. When traveling, be sure to record the days and times, events locations you visit as well as the emotions you had as well as the experiences you've had or experienced, etc. Make sure to take some photos to use to your journal entries.

Do not forget to record the lessons you've learned and what you enjoyed and did not like about the trip, any tips you've received, any suggestions you'd like to change and also your plans for the future.

Most importantly, keep an open mind when you travel. Be aware that biases can alter your perspective. A clear mind allows you to learn from new information, challenge your beliefs that are false, and come to different conclusions. That's what the growth mindset about: evolving when you experience changes.

Bullet Journal

Bullet journal (BuJo) was the idea by Ryder Carroll. It is designed to help you lead a more meaningful and fulfilling life. It includes:

* Index The index is located in the top in the notebook. It serves as an index and highlights the pages' page numbers and symbols in the notebook/journal. BuJo is a unique symbol for various things like the notes of events, projects prioritizing items, as well as ingenuous ideas and insights.

* Future log This is four-page piece which lists all your goals and travel plans, important birthdays, holidays, upcoming events, as well as long-term plans for the entire year. In this way, you'll be able to know what you'll be doing throughout the year in a single glance.

• Monthly Log: A log for the month is two-page spread. It includes an agenda that gives an eye-level view of every month it is. In this calendar, you can add details like your tasks for the month and other activities you may need to keep track of, such as finances and fitness or food items.

Daily log The daily log contains your daily to-do lists.

Bullet journaling helps you make plans instead of leaving things until an unexpected moment. As you are aware, habits like procrastination and disorder affect your relationships as well as your goals and projects. So planning ahead and doing the things you set out to complete will allow you to achieve success in your life.

The various types of journals we've covered in this chapter are all focused on one particular part of the life you lead. But, you may also choose to write about your experiences throughout the day and concentrate on what you're faced with in the course of your journal.

As mentioned earlier, there is one thing you need to incorporate into your journaling practices regardless of what else is happening in your life. It is the creation of an action plan.

The Benefits of Creating A To-Do List

Each day, you'll be faced with a range of tasks. If you're faced with a handful of tasksto complete, doing them effectively and in a timely manner shouldn't be a problem, provided you don't let distractions hinder you from completing the task at hand.

However when you are working on lots of work to do it can be difficult managing your workload and you may find yourself working all night to complete your task even when the majority tasks are distractions.

To-do lists can help you determine what tasks you must do first, and which do not require a significant amount in your day. When you create a to-do list it is important to consider the category that the tasks are placed into so you will know which tasks will allow you to advance in your life.

According to Eisenhower's principle, there are four types of work. These are:

* Urgent and important Important and urgent tasks: These are the ones you have put off until last minute and can't ignore or

unexpected situations that pop up every now and then.

Important, however not essential: These jobs are the ones that aid you in completing important work and meet your goals in your career and personal life. They might not be urgent however if you don't complete them in time, you might be rushing to finish these tasks later.

* Not crucial But urgent jobs are not urgent, but they're not essential in the sense that they don't help you achieve your goals. They usually involve performing tasks to help others. If you take on such tasks, they can hinder you from achieving your goals since they prevent you from taking on important tasks. You must delegate or shift the tasks you are assigned.

* Not urgent or important These are usually distractions. They're not important or urgent tasks. Often they involve performing favors to others. These tasks aren't contributing to the desired results you want to achieve. Therefore, it is best to be as adamant as is possible.

When you've got your priorities set, you can start to tackle the most important and urgent ones first before proceeding to other tasks you have on your list. If you do this, by the end of the day, you'll be able to say that you've completed what you needed to complete instead of getting distracted by tasks that you don't have to complete right now, or in any way.

Writing a to-do list has various benefits. They include:

#: Less anxiety

One of the biggest advantages of creating an agenda is that it lessens anxiety. Consider it.

If you're overwhelmed by the amount of work to complete and you're feeling overwhelmed as you're not sure what to do first. A list of tasks will help you determine the tasks you have to tackle first. It provides you with a sense of order and reduces anxiety.

A checklist of things to do also makes sure that you've got a checklist of the various tasks you'll have to accomplish. As long as you stick to the checklist carefully it will be easy to not be concerned about not doing something that is essential to your development. If you've outlined the steps you must follow to finish your task, you'll feel less stressed as you complete the steps knowing that at the conclusion of the process you'll have completed the task.

Many people notice that they feel less stressed when they make their list of things to do the previous night. If you create your to-do list prior to bed and your brain is aware there is a strategy in place for the day ahead. You might have a number of tasks to complete and accomplish, but creating a list gives you some peace as it helps create a sense that you are in control of your day.

If you get up in the morning rather than trying to think of all the things you'll need to remember you'll already have a plan. This means you'll be able to start taking on your work as quickly as you can. This will help you to make your day more productive.

Better organization

146

A list of tasks allows you to manage one task following the next. Instead of a maze of work, you can arrange your tasks according to their importance and priority. By doing this, you can make your life more organized. It can also be beneficial in other areas of your daily life.

In the various ways, some assignments you'll have to do belong to the urgent or urgent categories. When you think about it there are some tasks that could be tasks that you could have completed in the past however, since you didn't, you are forced to finish them now.

A daily list of tasks will assist you in completing the tasks you need to take care of prior to them becoming urgent. For instance, if have a task that must be completed towards the end of your month having a to-do list will help you plan your project ahead of time. It will allow you to work on certain aspects of the task, and by the end this month, you'll have completed the entire project. So, instead of hurrying to finish it at the last minute it's only necessary to finish the project before handing it over.

If you manage each task in this way your life will be in order and you'll be able to devote to other pursuits.

Productivity increase

Certain tasks you complete are repetitive. If you write a task list, you'll be able to figure out ways to accomplish these chores. For instance, you could discover it easier to complete your chores in a specific sequence or to complete your tasks according to a particular routine.

This is something you figure out after you've been doing it for some time. As time passes through, you get better at completing tasks on your list more quickly, because these tasks has become routine.

There's a benefit that comes with this.

You'll be less distracted in the course of your work since your ability to complete the tasks will improve. This means that you'll have free time to use this time for you or your loved ones. The extra time to unwind and enjoy life. This can put you in a better position to deal with any problems that arise in your daily life.

#: Better focus

Have you ever had so many things to accomplish that at the end of the day you decided to just do nothing? This is what occurs when there's no strategy that will help you tackle your work. The tasks you're assigned seem so overwhelming that you think that you'd rather take the day off or watching TV. This kind of attitude can hinder you from working toward your objectives.

But having a list of things to do will help you concentrate on the work at the moment. This is the issue. When you're creating a to-do list, you don't write down the amount of work you'll have to accomplish. It also outlines the time you'll need for each task. So, when you're working on the task at hand it is possible to focus on your task in the confidence that you've allotted time to complete the next job.

Instead of thinking about the various tasks you need to complete during the day, focus on the task that you must complete within an hour. This helps you focus better and allows you to work at the task until you've completed all them.

Improved motivation

As you begin to tackle the tasks on your list checklist, you might think that you've got a lot to complete, and this might be the case. However, when you have completed one task you are able to eliminate off the to-do list.

If, for instance, you had ten items that you wanted to complete, and you end up with nine things to complete, and when you've completed another job, you'll eliminate this task off your list. As time passes the work you've completed will exceed the tasks you have left.

The fact that every step you take gets you closer to finishing every task on the to-do-list gives you the motivation to get to the next step. Motivation like this is crucial because it stems from the things that you can quantify. The accomplishments you've made are the evidence you require to be able to prove that the work you're doing is effective. This means you'll be more likely to stay on the path to achieving your goals.

There's a second option you can try.

You could reward yourself for completing the tasks that are on your list of things to do. For instance, you could choose that you will reward yourself with a cup coffee upon completing a specific amount of tasks. The reward you receive will encourage you to complete the tasks in order you are able to take advantage of the reward.

#: Improved delegation

One thing you're advised to delegate some tasks. Things that are urgent however, they are acceptable to transfer to a competent person. If you do not have a list of the tasks you'd like to complete, it will be difficult to determine what tasks to delegate.

A to-do list can do more than just allow you to be able to keep track of all things to do; it can also help you to track your progress with every task. In this way, when you assign a task to someone else, you'll be aware of who you've assigned the task and when you're expecting them to finish the task. This is crucial as it helps avoid confusion particularly when you're involved in a team project.

It's incredibly disappointing to not complete a task due to the fact that you didn't assign some of the work to anyone else or because you were relying on someone else to finish the task before you could take on your task and the person didn't meet the deadline.

A list of tasks will help you determine what must be done prior to the accomplishment of the other tasks will follow. If you make a to-do list it is possible to set realistic deadlines for the tasks, and also follow-up with those who are required to complete the task.

#: Improved self-esteem

It's normal to feel proud on the work you've completed This is especially true in the past if you've struggled in completing specific tasks. A to-do list divides into several tasks. Consider the tasks in the same way as milestones. If you can complete an assignment, you'll have confidence feeling confident that you've done it correctly.

Getting the things done that are on your list of things to do gives you the feeling that you've done a great job and improves confidence in yourself. When the day is over instead of being sad and dissatisfied, you'll be satisfied that you managed to accomplish the task that you had set your sights to complete. After you've seen the benefits to a list of things to do and a positive attitude, your outlook will shift to one that is more positive.

If you're confronted having a lot of work to do instead of becoming overwhelmed and ready to give up before you begin the task, you'll take the moment to look at the task in a critical manner before breaking it into smaller tasks. Once you've completed the task, you'll feel satisfied with the work you've completed.

Peace of mind

There are times in life that need extra caution in order to complete specific tasks. For instance, if intend to take your vacation, you'll be looking to ensure that you are prepared with everything you require and depart your house in secure conditions.

A checklist of everything you'll need to bring will assist you in completing each item one at a time and give you peace of mind knowing that you can travel knowing that you've got everything that you'll need.

The same principles are applicable to the development of a strategy for special occasions like weddings. A list of things to do will help you plan for these events in a timely manner. It helps you avoid late-night rushes, which can lead to trying to complete too many tasks in an hour.

The knowledge that you've planned everything to the highest standard can ease your shoulders and allows you to relax and enjoy living your life, not worrying about the things you need to have completed.

A list of tasks is an effective tool can be used to organize the tasks you need to complete to complete them to the best of your abilities. The method of writing is the key to success. Therefore, do not be afraid to try it.

Chapter 9: The Reasons To Keep A Journal

If we could begin and end our day each day, with a trustworthy person who was willing to listen our every need for hours, our lives is more peaceful. While we might not have an ally like that but you can if you decide to journal. Writing a journal and keeping one differs. In the diary, you generally simply record the events that took place and the details about an event, but when you journal, you note down your deepest and most genuine thoughts, your goals and desires, your fears and anxieties--it's a record of all of it. Journaling is a way to express yourself without having to have to try to portray yourself as an individual, as the more authentic that you can be, the greater the benefit of your journaling is for you. Here are some reasons you should begin journaling.

Journaling saves you time

Journaling can help you save time to think and be more productive. If you share what you are thinking and feeling early in early morning hours, you release yourself of anxiety, worries, regrets and other emotional issues and provide you with an emotional and clear slate to begin your day on. Journalists who write early in the day are able to concentrate on their tasks and not worry about interruptions. They also have greater energy and become more productive.

Journaling is similar to talking to the therapy

Therapy is expensive, and journaling could provide the same level of experience for the cost of a pen and notebook. If you write every day you gain knowledge and enhance your self-awareness. You are more aware of the world around you, and this helps build your empathy towards others. Write down the good things happening in your life and also the difficulties and struggles you're experiencing.

Journaling can boost confidence in yourself.

When you feel doubtful about yourself, journaling can provide you the self-confidence you'll need. Note your achievements and achievements, as well as your successes and even big or small wins within your journals. Recording them all down is extremely helpful especially when you're feeling low or depressed.

Writing can be a way to let some old items go.

Journaling can help you face the past that has been weighing you back. If you're feeling you need to share your feelings about a particular event or even say something that is difficult to someone else You can write everything about the experience in your journal since you don't want anyone to know about it. Writing down everything you want to say is likely to ease your burden and help you gain an understanding and clarity of the issue. If you can gain the clarity you require, you'll be better able to decide the best course of action to address your concerns.

Journaling encourages you

Journals are the ideal space to record all your dreams, goals and goals. Record them all down and also how you'll get there. Positive affirmations can go a great distance.

Journaling can be fun.

Journaling can be enjoyable and we've all experienced the positive benefits of being in a position to laugh and smile at yourself. It is not necessary to remain serious all the time.

Journaling allows you to have the opportunity to reconnect with yourself

If you're not sure how to reconnect with yourself, writing in your journal is your solution. Within your journals, you'll write about your personal prayers and express your gratitude and even ask for assistance. Note not only what's on your mind but also what's going on in your heart, too.

Journaling helps preserve memories

Sometimes, photographs aren't enough. While you may be able to recall the location and time when the photo was taken, in many cases, the meaning behind the photograph is not remembered. If something positive or even negative occurs to you, you should write about the event. Write down the details as well as the way you were feeling about it. When you record the details of what happened to you, you'll forever remember the events as if they happened in the past. If you keep a journal you'll never have to worry about losing a single moment of your life.

Journaling improves your writing

Journaling can help you naturally develop your writing. Writing more often, you'll improve will get. Also, consistently making entries in your journals can simplify writing. Even if you're writing just for your own use journals can aid in building muscles you can apply to different types of writing.

Journaling helps sharpen your senses

If you write regularly about your thoughts and experiences and experiences, you become more attentive. If you decide to express your thoughts on something you are more focused on it. In addition, you get into the habit of paying attention to the smallest details in your everyday life. This means that you sharpen your eyes and can see the world with greater clarity.

Journaling is beneficial for many reasons.

It was commonplace to keep a journal or a personal journal before the advent of cell phones and computers invented. But, because of technology, only a small number of people are now keeping a journal and very few people understand the value and importance of keeping a journal. Being in a position to write and read quickly gives you access to the most powerful source of personal growth and power. Many people claim they don't have the time to write, but you do not require a lot of time to keep a diary. Just by taking only a few minutes of time each day to write down what you are feeling you can reap the many benefits of writing such as the ones below.

Journals can assist you in establishing specific goals. When you record your goals and what you want to achieve every day the ideas will be clearer and you'll be able to see the tasks you're required to complete that are worth your time and energy. In writing the thoughts you have and ideas, you will have a more clarity about the things you truly want to achieve in life.

Journals can make your life easier. When you take note of your thoughts, accomplishments concerns, as well as thanks you'll be able to manage your life in a systematic manner. Because you will have a better understanding about your life, you'll be aware of what you have to accomplish and will find it easier to deal with the whims of life. If you record things in a notebook you'll see your life becoming more organised and less complicated.

Journals can be a great way to improve your relationships with others. Journaling gives you the chance to think about the things you must do, particularly during times of stress or personal problems. Because you'll be able to write all that you have to say through your journals, you'll discover how to be more understanding with your family and friends, and not hurt them by your words.

Journals helps you to make yourself more attractive. If you are aware of your self and accept what you are, regardless of flaws and imperfections You'll feel more confident and more adept in expressing yourself.

Journals can be a great way to motivate you. With your journals, you could write about all the things you'd like to accomplish and all the things you wish to become. If you continue to write and read positive affirmations, you'll provide yourself with the motivation and inspiration you require to achieve your goals.

A journal can act as a proof of the truth of your experience. If you record your experiences in life and your experience, you can give greater significance to your experience.

A journal can offer you the peace and quiet you require. Our lives are busy and full of anxiety, and if you don't take your time in silence you'll be easily overwhelmed, and your goals in life can become blurred. Journaling can be a type of meditation as it helps you to shut out your thoughts and focus in your thinking.

Journals can help you express yourself. Most people can't communicate fully, even to their closest of acquaintances. The release of feelings that are difficult to express is possible through writing in the form of a journal.

How do I begin journaling?

Journaling is a fantastic method to build more discipline, since it makes you more attentive and aware of your behavior. If you're looking to eat healthier, keeping the food diary is a excellent method of paying attention to the foods you consume and help to eat healthier. Also, keeping a record of the good things happening in your life will aid in identifying the positive patterns that you observe in your life. let go of the negatives can help to focus your attention in things that will enrich your time and energy.

If you have chose to keep your journal The next step is to select the appropriate journaling medium you will use. There are many alternatives to choose from. Be sure to pick the one that you're more comfortable. Don't be concerned about what could be a good fit for someone else but you must choose the one that is most suitable for you. Here are a few choices:

* Notebooks. Many people find it enjoyable to physically record your thoughts, feelings and ideas in the paper of a notebook. Notebooks can offer you complete control over the content you'd like to record and also provides the

greatest privacy as it's extremely unlikely it'll be lost or stolen. But the drawback to having a notebook is that in the event that it is lost, you'll not have any backups. That means all the notes you've made is deleted for all time.

* Unique notebooks. If you aren't motivated to write in a simple notebook, search for notebooks with unique designs filled with tasks, notes and short quotations which can assist you in writing about the day and how you are feeling at the moment. Unique notebooks will help you by asking questions such as, "What are you grateful for today?", "What exciting moment happened to you today?", etc.

* Journaling apps. If you're unable to keep yourself from your phone or laptop choose a journaling app which offer total protection and privacy. The best part about these apps is that they're extremely

accessible, and whenever you want to write down your thoughts or feelings you are able to do it easily.

* Text file. If you're finding it difficult to maintain an application or notebook, then you could keep an encrypted notepad or word file on your laptop. Remember, however it's more difficult to express yourself on phones or laptops since you are unable to draw or draw drawings.

* Blog. Blogging is a relatively new and effective method of gaining the advantages of journaling regardless of whether you're looking to make your name known or just using it as a way to communicate with others. Making your thoughts public on a blog will keep your blog open to the largest possible audience, however it is also a cost of security. If you're looking to test your hand at blogging you can find a variety of blogs hosting websites and tools you can test. You can even modify your blog to suit your

preferences to make it a complete image of who you are.

If you decide to start your journal, you'll always benefit from the advantages previously mentioned. It is not necessary to be a celebrity to have your thoughts be worthwhile. Journaling is for you and not for anybody other than you. Journaling can be a source of inspiration and provide a more clear perspective on your life.

Once you've decided on the medium you want to use, you can opt to keep it plain and straightforward or design it to suit the style you'd like. You can draw on it, make sketches, add pictures and quotes that will inspire you and so on. You are free to do whatever you like with your journal. You just need to create it as your own. Before you begin writing, be sure to note down the exact date as well as the time of the day and then start writing. Note down the things that occurred on that day, the ways

167

you participated in the events, and what you thought about the whole experience. Write about people who encouraged you, who were kind for you. Also, then write about the people who stifled you. If, at some point in your life, you came to the decision to write about the realization. If you suddenly felt the desire to leave your job or return to school Write about the decision. Let it go. Once you've completed your journal it is then you'll know the things you want to accomplish. Many people are bored after writing in journals. To ensure that you don't give up on journaling or becoming bored keep it to a minimum of 10 minutes daily. The goal is to ensure that you revisit your journal each day, even if it's only for one or two minutes, so that your task doesn't become repetitive.

Journaling doesn't have to be stressful. If you're just beginning your journey, begin with a small entry. There's no need to write an elaborate piece of work. Simply write the details or make a sketch. There is no need to follow a specific rule or follow a set of guidelines. The first time to create an entry may be boring. You may think you don't have anything to write about. However, when you begin to become more attentive because you wish to record your thoughts in your journal, you'll slowly become aware of the sheer amount of happenings around you every day. At first your journal, you can start by noting 3 things that made your be happy, or smile, five items you consumed or two things that made you feel inspired.

Choose the medium that most inspires and motivates you. Explore your expression on paper, your computer, or even using your mobile. Check out how you are using your senses, and decide the medium in which you are comfortable with when it comes to expressing yourself. Some people begin writing down their thoughts on blogs but then find themselves later using a pen and notebook, as they feel it is more relaxing. Explore your options and play around, making sure you're not limiting yourself when is time to be creative and free.

There's no right and wrong with journaling. What you write or do is not yours to control So, be willing the chance to fail, experiment on your own writing styles and try new things. The main goal is to put your thoughts into your notebook, blog or even a text document. It doesn't have to fit within the space or require a number or categorized, and it doesn't need to include an intro, body or conclusion.

If you've been journaling for a few months and are confident that you'll keep doing it, invest on your notebooks. Journals are where you can store your most personal emotions and precious memories. Therefore, it's best to purchase beautiful journals that will last for a long time and not be damaged.

Keep everything you can to keep in your journal. Even if you think your life is monotonous, the things that occur to you aren't always identical. If you get a surprising letter from a long-lost acquaintance Keep the letter. If you have a fascinating incident on the train on the way traveling to work, save the ticket stub and then write about the event in your journal. If you are compelled to share your thoughts and it doesn't interfere with your work, you should write it down. The faster you're in a position to let go of certain things and let them go, the better you'll be able to manage these issues.

Many people don't try journaling due to the assumption that they already know what's about to occur. Some people believe that journaling's benefits aren't true however if you don't attempt it, you'll never actually experience it. The best way to experience it is to give it a go. It is not necessary to feel overwhelmed by the process of writing entries every day. If you note down 1 or 2 phrases to summarize your day, it will have a significant impact in terms of clarity and understanding.

Tips for journaling to aid you

A journal will provide you with many advantages. It will help you improve your self-confidence and gain an understanding of your habits and actions. Writing can assist you in dealing with anxiety and stress, enhance your mental and physical well-being, enhance your connections with your friends and family and provide you with the inspiration and motivation you require Here are some of the tips for journaling that you can use:

Once you've decided to begin a journal, start your first entry by describing the current state of your life. Be honest about your feelings about your work as well as your current situation and the relationships you have. Consider whether the place you're at right today is where you would like to be.

Note down your thoughts in your journal for between 5 and 10 minutes per day. There's no need to create a novel or be overly elaborate, particularly when you're just beginning your journey. Write for five to ten minutes and allow your thoughts to flow. Don't be concerned about your grammar, or how stupid your thoughts could be.

A major part of journaling is helping you accept yourself what you are. One method to achieve this is to develop the habit of being grateful. Each time you write on your notebook, make sure you do not forget to create an inventory of things that you are thankful for. This can be extremely helpful in times of feeling unsatisfied or dissatisfied with where you're in life.

* Do not restrict your journal to only words. If you discover you are able to better convey yourself using images take advantage of it. Draw pictures, take photos or make use of colors.

* You will become more observant when you begin journaling. To increase your ability to observe you should be conscious of the surroundings and then write about it. Note down things that you observe.

Note all your achievements regardless of how large or small they are within your diary. When you're feeling discouraged then glance at them. They can be a reminder of your accomplishments and serve as your motivation to continue working toward your objectives.

* Songs are able to bring us back and trigger important moments. This is why it's important to include in your journal the songs you love or songs that you cherish. It's also better to record how you feel each

when you listen to those songs to allow you to go back to that particular moment in your life.

Write down any things that bother or bother you. If you record them, you'll be able disengage yourself from them and gain an entirely new perspective to enable you to let them go more easily.

Note down your worries thoughts, doubts, or questions and listen carefully for an answer. This will help you build your sense of intuition.

Write everything and anything you'd like to say. There's no need to consider the way to organize your journal. It is up to you what your journal will play whatever you want. Write about your best memories, write about your negative ones, share your frustrations, express your happiness, write about your accomplishments, and also share your concerns. Writing is an excellent method of releasing tension that has built up within your. If you write regularly the thoughts you have and your feelings as time passes, you'll develop an emotional development that will assist you in learning to deal with stress and challenges.

* You do not need to sit for hours within your notebook. It is only necessary to stick to it. Set it as a habit by setting a certain time in your day when you write it down. You could write it down when you get up and when you are going to bed at night. You can also decide to write it down whenever you feel having the desire to release your thoughts and emotions. The most important thing is to make moment to keep a journal.

In addition to writing down your thoughts and letting go of the emotions that you are feeling Your journal can also be an account of all your personal memories and experiences. To keep your journal interesting and useful, ensure you record all the details you want to include such as names, dates and locations as well as any other detail relevant. Do not assume that you'll recall the names of people or the incidents that occurred in the future when you revisit them. The initial writing of all the details might appear tedious, but eventually you'll be grateful for it in the future.

* Include random information to keep it exciting. Apart from the facts of an occasion or circumstance, write about your thoughts and feelings during the time it took place.

* Even if you stopped making notes in your journals for couple of days, don t get dissatisfied. You can pick up where started and record your thoughts and thoughts within your diary.

Keep notes wherever you go, but be sure to not lose or forget it. the journal because it holds all your most intimate thoughts and secrets. Carrying it with you wherever you go is helpful, particularly during times when you are overwhelmed or stressed.

* You do not need to be concerned about your grammar, spelling and punctuation marks. Write in the style you prefer or with the way you like spelling. You can let the rules be your guide right now. As you go you will learn what you would like your entries to appear and how you would like to arrange the entries.

* There are no limitations on what you can write about within your journals. You are able to write about your feelings and reactions to the events and situations that take place around you, your dreams that you wish to achieve or get an inspiration from, poems that makes you feel moved, photos or cutouts of magazines and

newspapers that you like or books that you'd like to read and music that brings to mind memories, websites you should investigate shopping lists, errands, grocery lists as well as other things. Whatever matters to you could record in your journal. Be sure to don't wait long before writing them down. Thoughts can arise anytime So every time you have an idea, a thought or an emotion that you cannot help but put down, record it immediately in your journal.

Don't complicate your journal. Keep it simple. There is no need to draw every entry. There is no need to alter the colors of your pen. There is no need to label all things. If you're feeling inspired today , and slow the next day, it is perfectly fine. Do what you like today.

* Make sure to keep your journal that allow people to easily gain accessibility to your journal. Journaling is something you

keep only for yourself, unless your intention was to communicate your experience with others via blogging, for instance. If you're keeping a journal just for to let your emotions flow, store it in a safe place. Journals are your personal space to write about whatever topic you'd like without fear of being assessed. If you start to fear that someone might read it and read it, you'll begin restricting your writing and the advantages of writing in journals will not be as efficient.

Write only when you are required to. Make a point of writing daily in your journal even if that means just writing a few words to express your day. Don't go into great of detail if it doesn't think you should. Since if you don't enjoy what you're currently doing there's a good chance that you'll never want to do it in the first place. Set aside 10 minutes every day to write a journal. If you're unable to write anything regarding your experience, be honest about how you're feeling. Make an effort to record your thoughts daily in your journal. Writing can make you feel great and not cause you to feel guilty when you don't have anything to write about.

* If you don't have anything you want to talk about simply make note of the time, date and place and then write about the surroundings you're in. Write about it if you would like to, write down the elements that are uplifting or write down your feelings about it. Do you love it or dislike it? Are you looking to change something about it? Start with these issues to assist you in getting your mind warmed up and provide you with an idea of what you can do to start journaling.

Find the ideal moment and time when you feel the urge to writing. Apart from writing in it whenever you feel the need to do so, you should set the time in your day that you want to write. It could take a few days and some experimentation before you discover the ideal date and time you'll be able to see the importance of it for you.

* In contrast to our essay, term paper and school papers Journaling is focused on the amount of words and not what you wrote. Don't stress over the funnyness of your writing or how poorly you wrote your thoughts. Nobody cares. It's important you write about the issues. If you're struggling to get over issues with spelling, grammar, and punctuation, write fast. If you write fast and write, you'll minimize distractions and remove the voices telling you that you're wrong.

If you prefer blogging and not write, it's totally fine. Typing on a computer is certainly faster and more efficient however, from time to the time, try writing with your hands. Writing the thoughts of your heart and emotions utilizes the different parts that your mind than writing. Before you start arguing about feeling exhausted while using your hands to write, bear in your mind that journaling isn't about quantity, the quantity of wordswritten or efficacy. It's about being able to convey the thoughts of your heart and emotions, and writing in hand lets you be more connected. Allow your mind to relax and take in the experience. Allow your brain to process all the thoughts running through it.

* You don't have to inform anyone that you're writing. Keep journaling as a private thing. If no one knows you're writing, there's nothing that you need to be concerned about. There is no pressure to write, and the more stressful the process will feel.

* You are aware that you do not have to be concerned about others criticizing the content you wrote however, it is important to be aware that you must let

your judgment and criticism in the past. No matter what you wrote or wrote, you must accept it. You should not erase it or tear the paper then begin on a fresh page. Don't worry about it. If your writing isn't great is fine. If you think your story is silly, why should you care?